INTRODUCTION TO

Dog Agility

Margaret H. Bonham

Filled with Full-color Photographs
Illustrations by Michele Earle-Bridges

BARRON'S

Dedication

To Larry, for his constant support. To Snopeak Kiana of Sky Warrior NA, CGC, U-AGI, WPD, WTD, "Kiana," who taught me more about training than any other dog. In Memory of Keyokuk's Arctic Wind CGC, WTP, WPD, and Aunt Susan Bonham Briggs, an ardent dog lover.

All inquiries should be addressed to:
Barron's Educational Series, Inc.
250 Wireless Boulevard
Hauppauge, New York 11788
http://www.barronseduc.com

International Standard Book No. 0-7641-1439-5
Library of Congress Catalog Card No. 00-036280

Library of Congress Cataloging-in-Publication Data
Bonham, Margaret H.
    Introduction to dog agility / Margaret H. Bonham.
        p. cm.
    Includes bibliographical references (p.   ).
    ISBN 0-7641-1439-5 (alk. paper)
    1. Dogs—Agility trials. 2. Dogs—Training. I. Title.
SF425.4 .B66   2000
636.7´0888—dc21   00-036280

Printed in China
9 8 7

Legal Disclosures

USDAA®, Agility Dog®, Advanced Agility Dog®, Master Agility Dog®, Agility Dog Champion®, Snooker Master^{SM}, Gamblers Master^{SM}, Relay Master^{SM}, Jumpers Master^{SM}, Performance Dogs^{SM}, Performance Dog II^{SM}, Performance Dog III^{SM}, Performance Snooker^{SM}, Performance Gambler^{SM}, Performance Jumper^{SM}, Accomplished Performance Dog^{SM}, Veteran Agility Dog^{SM}, Veteran Advanced Agility Dog^{SM}, Veteran Master Agility Dog^{SM}, Veteran Performance Dog^{SM}, Veteran Gambler^{SM}, Veteran Snooker^{SM}, Veteran Jumper^{SM}, Junior Handler—Beginner Agility^{SM}, Junior Handler—Elementary Agility^{SM}, Junior Handler—Intermediate Agility^{SM}, Junior Handler—Senior Agility^{SM}, Agility Top Ten^{SM}, Grand Prix of Dog Agility^{SM}, Dog Agility Masters®, Dog Agility SteepleChase^{SM}, and Spring Festival of Dog Agility^{SM} are all registered trademarks and exclusive service marks of the United States Dog Agility Association.

Disclaimers

This dog agility training manual tells the reader how to train a dog in the sport of dog agility. The author and the publisher consider it important to point out that the advice given in the book is meant primarily for normally developed dogs from a reputable breeder; that is, dogs of excellent physical health and good temperament.

Anyone who adopts a fully grown dog should be aware that the animal has already formed its basic impressions of human beings. The new owner should watch the dog carefully, including its behavior toward humans, and should meet the previous owner. If the dog comes from a shelter, it may be possible to get some information on the dog's background and peculiarities.

There are dogs that, for whatever reason, behave in an unnatural manner, or may even bite. Under no circumstances should a known "biter" or an otherwise ill-tempered dog be adopted or purchased as a pet or agility prospect.

Caution is further advised in the association of children with dogs, in meeting with other dogs, and in exercising a dog without a leash.

Even well-behaved and carefully supervised dogs sometimes do damage to someone else's property or cause accidents. It is therefore in the owner's interest to be adequately insured against such eventualities.

Consult a professional trainer if your dog shows any sign of aggression. Do not attempt to correct aggression without help from a professional. Even normal or gentle dogs may bite due to fear or pain. While the author has made every attempt to warn the reader of possible situations, the responsibility lies with the reader to prevent situations that may occur that would lead to a dog biting.

The veterinary advice in this book is meant as a guide and is not a substitute for your veterinarian. Consult your veterinarian in the event of an emergency and in overall routine health care. Certain procedures within this text can cause serious injury or death if performed improperly. Consult a veterinarian if you are not familiar with the procedures.

Likewise, while the author has tried to take every possible precaution in advising the reader in safety, the sport of dog agility can be hazardous. Accidents can and do sometimes occur that may result in serious injury or death. Always take precautions to avoid accidents and injury.

Photo Credits
Kent and Donna Dannen

Illustrations
Michele Earle-Bridges

Contents

Acknowledgments

The author would like to acknowledge the following people, dogs, and organizations for their help with this book:

- The American Kennel Club (AKC), The North American Dog Agility Council (NADAC), the United Kennel Club (UKC), the United States Dog Agility Association (USDAA), and the American Agility Associates Inc. (AAAI), Pet's Control and the Aurora Dog Agility Club, both in Aurora, Colorado.
- Reviewers: Laurence J. Bonham, Betty M. Holowinski, Kenneth Tatsch (USDAA), Heather Smith (USDAA), Laura Gummelt (USDAA), Nancy Matlock (AKC), Sharon Anderson (AKC), Becky Woodruff (NADAC), Beth Godwin, Joni Weed, Debby Funk, Kathy Bourland, Liz Durfee, and Marilu Baskin (AAAI).
- The following owners and dogs: Shelley Bowman and "Lilac" (Always BWitchn Lilac Bookay CGC HIC); Joni Weed and "Beaujolias" (U-CD, U-AGII Reidsan Ebony Beaujolais OSO CDX, AX, NAJ, NAC, NAG); Deanna Clawson and "Maya" (Yatahah Maya); Eydie Hoeppner and "Xena" (Xena Willingham NA); Kim Horsley and "Becket" (U-AGI Ragtyme Talkin Up a Storm CD, AX, OAS); Kathy Lester and "Jeffrey" (U-AGI, AHBA-HTDI CH. Mihran Black Tie Optional AX OAJ HS); Cindy Macklin of Jump and Go Mountain Agility and "Paisley" (MX, MXJ, MAD, CGC), "Aspen" (OA, CGC), and "Willow" (OA, HS, AD); Kim Gillaspie and "Luna" (Lil Lunatig Shake-Rat-N-Roll CD, AX, AXJ, CGC, AD); Tracy Lorraine Smith and "Impi" (U-ACH, CH. Norelka City Slicker, CD, AX, AXJ, AD, OAC, OGC, NJC, SAD), and "Karoo" (U-ACH Karoo of Injasuti CDX, AX, AXJ, AD, OAC, NGC, OJC, SAD); and Carol Panning of Pet's Control/RocWind Canine Center and "Stetson" (Ch. Sundance Stetson CD).
- Dr. Annette Stumf, DVM for constant technical support. Dr. Arleigh J. Reynolds, DVM and Dr. Gregory A. Rinehart, DVM, whose work has greatly influenced portions of this text.
- Mark Miele, Managing Editor at Barron's and Deborah Schneider, the best agent one could have.
- Snopeak Kiana of Sky Warrior NA, CGC, U-AGI, WTD, WPD, who got me involved in agility.
- Susan Conant for encouragement and emotional support.

PART ONE

WHERE TO START

Chapter 1

A Sport for Everyone

Agility is a sport that has wowed audiences since its inception in 1978 at the Crufts Dog Show in England. John Varley and Peter Meanwell had devised a kind of steeplechase for dogs intended as entertainment for the spectators between events. Instead, what they had developed was a brand new sport for all dog lovers.

Agility came "across the pond" and in 1986, Kenneth Tastch founded the United States Dog Agility Association (USDAA) in Texas. In 1986, other agility organizations were quick to follow, including the American Agility Associates (AAAI) in Colorado founded by Bob and Marilu Baskin and the National Council for Dog Agility (NCDA) founded by Bud Kramer in Kansas. The two major purebred registries, the American Kennel Club (AKC) and the United Kennel Club (UKC), appeared in the mid 1990s. North American Dog Agility Council (NADAC) was founded in 1993 by a group headed by Sharon Nelson.

What is all this excitement about agility? Agility is fun. Dogs that would normally be bored by the repetition of obedience suddenly have a new and exciting sport that demands intelligence, speed, and teamwork. Handler and dog quickly become a team as the handler directs the dog over hurdles, through tunnels, and over a variety of contact obstacles. As the dog and han-

dler progress through the levels, courses become more complex with traps, call-offs, and abrupt turns. The time factor shrinks. Watching a master in dog agility is a real treat.

Agility is not just for the purebred. While AKC only allows purebred in competition, USDAA, NADAC (North American Dog Agility Council), and UKC all allow mixed-breeds to compete for titles. Nor is agility an exclusive club for the able-bodied. UKC has special concessions for handicapped handlers. All you need is a healthy dog.

What Is Agility?

Agility is where dogs compete on an obstacle course for the best times. When people do not understand what dog agility is all about, I give them the brief explanation that agility is a "steeplechase for dogs" or a "doggie obstacle course." Of course, agility has more than just jumps and takes more finesse than a simple obstacle course, but it is sometimes easier to put it in such terms. Agility requires intense teamwork between the dog and her handler.

A judge sets up a course, normally consisting of contact obstacles, tunnels, jumps, and other obstacles and times the dog as the dog and handler make their way through the course. Missed obstacles, knocked down bars, improperly performed obstacles, run-outs, fly-offs, and other hazards can severely penalize or disqualify the run. Jump heights and course times depend on the dog's height at the withers.

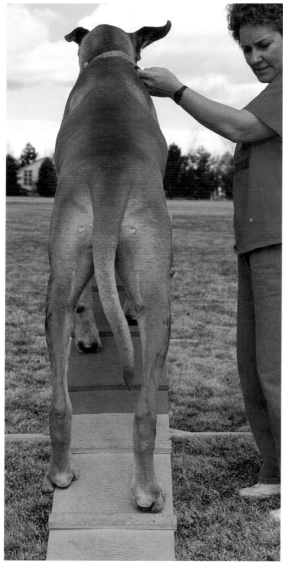

Even big dogs enjoy the sport of dog agility.

The Fab Four: AKC, NADAC, UKC, and USDAA

At the time of this writing, there are four major agility-sanctioning bodies within the United States: AKC, NADAC, UKC, and USDAA. USDAA first appeared in the mid and late 1980s; whereas, AKC, NADAC, and UKC sanctioning did not occur until the mid 1990s. Other agility organizations include ASCA (Australian Shepherd Club of America) and AAC (Agility Association of Canada).

Each organization has something to offer. (Certainly a multi-titled dog, if nothing else!) Dogs that compete for titles in each organization can receive titles in the equivalent of novice, intermediate, expert, and masters classes. There are special classes as well such as Jumpers with Weaves (JWW) in AKC and Jumpers, Gamblers, Snooker, and Relay in USDAA.

USDAA and NADAC follow the British agility rules more closely. USDAA tends to be faster with higher jumps. NADAC has lower jumps and flowing courses but similar rules to USDAA. AKC has lower jumps and slower times than USDAA, allowing more breeds to earn titles. UKC has lower jumps and longer times, but emphasizes accuracy and handling over speed. NADAC has a special Veteran's class for older dogs and handlers with lower jump heights and a longer course time for dogs over seven years old or handlers over 60. Likewise, USDAA has a Performance class that enables dogs that would have difficulty competing in the Championship Program to obtain titles with lower jumps, lower A-frame, and slightly longer course times.

Both USDAA and NADAC also have a Junior Handler program that enable those under eighteen to compete for titles and focuses on working as a team.

Benefits of Agility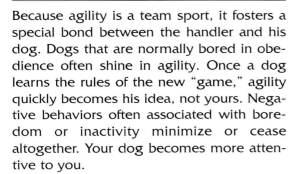

Because agility is a team sport, it fosters a special bond between the handler and his dog. Dogs that are normally bored in obedience often shine in agility. Once a dog learns the rules of the new "game," agility quickly becomes his idea, not yours. Negative behaviors often associated with boredom or inactivity minimize or cease altogether. Your dog becomes more attentive to you.

This does not happen overnight, however. Agility is not a quick fix for behavior problems. You can't attend two or three classes and expect Ace will stop digging in the garden or chewing on your furniture. Agility focuses on you and your bond with your dog. If the bond is not very good right now, agility done properly will strengthen that bond over time. As you begin to enjoy your dog's company, you may find yourself including Ace in more outings. In some ways, agility may be training you more than the dog!

Agility is wonderful for the timid or unsure dog if introduced gently. Once a timid dog discovers he can do a particular obstacle and obtain praise, the dog's confidence builds. You may bring about a whole new dimension to Ace's personality neither you nor Ace knew existed.

A Border Collie performing weave poles in a sequence.

An exceedingly long Bouvier? No, just a couple of dogs having fun with agility!

A Golden Retriever negotiates the A-frame.

The author's Alaskan Malamute, Kiana, negotiates an UKC obstacle called the swing plank.

metropolitan area or town, there is likely to be agility clubs or training facilities close by. (Even if you live in a rural area, you may find agility equipment and trainers within a reasonable distance.) Join a club or take a class (usually offered through obedience training facilities). If you are not sure who is in your area that practices agility, contact the national organizations or if you have web access, go to *www.dogpatch.org*, where you can look up various trials and matches by state. Every match and trial has contact names for the trial. Through the trial secretary, you should be able to find a local

Agility is a great way for your dog to get in shape. If your dog is a chronic couch potato, agility will increase his activity level and get him in shape.

Most of all, agility is fun. The sheer joy of watching a dog as he rushes around the course and performs obstacles is worth the hours of training. Your dog will love it too. It will make him feel useful and give him something to look forward to each week. It will build a team bond between you, and it will give him the joy in learning and accomplishing new things.

How to Get Started

You don't have to construct or purchase costly agility equipment. If you live near a

Xena, the Bulldog, enjoys the challenge of agility.

Agility provides a challenge for both the dog and owner and fosters teamwork.

club or organization you can become involved in.

If you are a great distance from any agility clubs or training facilities, you may wish to construct a few simple agility pieces and see if you like it before taking the plunge and purchasing or building costly equipment. Chapter 11 provides a few ideas for inexpensive and simple agility obstacles that you can build or obtain with minimal effort and cost. These at-home agility pieces are great for owners who wish to practice certain obstacles or sequencing.

Chapter 2

Is Your Dog Ready for Agility?

Choosing a Dog for Agility

Author's note: to avoid using the impersonal "it" when referring to a dog, I have chosen the names "Ace" and "Sierra."

Turning Ace into Ace Agile Dog

You don't need a special dog to compete in agility. If you are a pet owner, your next competition dog may be sitting beside you. If your dog is healthy and able to learn a few simple commands, maybe Ace is actually Ace Agile Dog.

Ace does not have to be a particular age, although Ace should still be active and healthy. NADAC, for example, has a Veteran's class in which you can run dogs over seven years old with lower jump heights and longer times. Although breed differences set puppies at different ages, puppies younger than a year should not jump regulation heights as it puts too much stress on developing joints and bones. If you own one of the larger breeds that mature slowly

(e.g., Alaskan Malamutes, Bernese Mountain Dogs, St. Bernards, or Great Danes), you should probably wait until a year and a half to two years before stressing the dog's joints with frequent jumping. All national agility organizations mentioned here have age limits for younger dogs to prevent injuring or possibly crippling a dog that is not fully grown. For those who have larger breed puppies, the good news is you will be able to train other obstacles, although you should not jump the puppy frequently or at regulation height. You have your puppy's entire lifetime ahead of it—be

TIP: Finding a reputable breeder or breed rescue

Contact the AKC at (919) 233-9767 or visit their website at www.akc.org for breed club contact information. Most national breed clubs have breeder referral services and affiliated rescue organizations. The breeder referral services will refer breeders who are in good standing with the national club. You will still need to screen the breeders for guarantees and health certifications.

Any dog can do agility, even a Great Dane like Stetson. Of course, the tunnel is a tight fit!

Purebred Versus Mixed Breed

The following chart shows which agility organizations you may compete in and obtain titles from if you have a registered purebred, a purebred with a special registration such as an ILP or LP, a registered mixed breed (an LP from UKC), or an unregistered purebred or mixed breed. Note: regardless of the pedigree, all dogs need to be registered within the respective agility organization.

	Registered	Special Registration	Unregistered
Purebred	AKC	AKC (ILP)	NADAC
	NADAC	UKC (LP)	USDAA
	UKC	NADAC	
	USDAA	USDAA	
Mixed Breed	NADAC	UKC (LP)	NADAC
	USDAA	NADAC	USDAA
	USDAA		

patient, the puppy will quickly become an adult.

Any breed can do agility. Even mixed breeds are allowed to compete against purebreds in NADAC, UKC, and USDAA trials. If you have an unregistered purebred (a dog you adopted from rescue, for instance), you can register your dog for a special registration in AKC and UKC and compete for obedience, agility, and tracking titles. UKC has a special registration known as AMBOR for mixed breeds. In both AKC and UKC, dogs with these special registrations must be neutered. USDAA and NADAC have no such limitations.

All agility organizations have different jump heights so height should not be an issue. Yorkshire Terriers, Chihuahuas, Jack Russell Terriers, and even Basset Hounds compete in agility. AKC, NADAC, and UKC provide extra time for smaller dogs, being aware that smaller dogs must take more steps than the bigger guys. Likewise, in AKC the dogs in the larger classes may get a second or two more because their course is technically longer. Alaskan Malamutes, Bernese Mountain Dogs, and Great Danes have all done agility with success. NADAC has a jump height exemption list for big or deep-chested dogs.

The ideal agility conformation (starting at shoulder, clockwise)—shoulder should be approximately 30 degrees and well-angulated—chest should be egg-shaped—tail should be set low, hips powerful and well-angulated—pasterns should not be too long or short—elbows should be flat against chest—feet should be compacted and arched, not splayed.

Even Bassets can do agility.

If you are a multi-dog household, choosing a dog for agility may be a daunting task. Choose the dog you've had the most training success with or the one that you would be willing to work with. Or you can train them all—many handlers have successfully trained their housepets.

Obtaining a Dog for Agility

Start with your own dog, if this is your first time training in agility. Do not purchase a dog for the sole intent of using it for agility and then discover you don't like agility and don't want the dog. This is clearly irresponsible. You should consider any dog you adopt or purchase to be your dog for life, whether it turns out to be a competitive dog or just a pet. Many fine dogs with wonderful temperaments may not make top agility competitors, due to speed limitations or limitations in attitude.

If you are looking for another dog, and would like to have a dog that may have an edge over others in agility, certain breeds do have a tendency toward being more successful. These are the herding breeds such as the Border Collie, the Pembroke Welsh Corgi, the Australian Shepherd, and the Shetland Sheepdog. The Golden Retriever, although not a herding breed, deserves mention as well. Note that this is a generalization and that many other breeds produce awesome agility competitors.

A Puli jumps in an agility trial.

Likewise, some herding dogs have proven dismal failures in agility.

If you do decide to find a pet that may make an agile dog, consider adopting a dog out of rescue or the local shelter. You'll be saving a dog's life plus giving it attention and confidence through agility training. You can register an unregistered purebred with AKC and UKC provided you fill out the necessary paperwork, provide photographs, and neuter the dog. Mixed breeds can compete in NADAC, UKC, and USDAA trials, so do not rule the loveable mutt out.

Perhaps you are looking for a puppy or a dog out of certain lines. Contact a reputable breeder who is familiar with agility and request her help in selecting a puppy. Note that a puppy will take a year or more before it is ready to compete in agility. Both parents of the puppy should have their OFA certification and prove clear of hip and elbow dysplasia. Both parents should have their CERF (eye) certification. The breeder should specify whether you are purchasing a pet or show quality dog. (Show quality dogs are much more expensive than pet quality and usually the faults that make the dog pet quality will not interfere with its ability to do agility.) The breeder should have a contract guaranteeing the puppy's health and temperament and should state in the contract that she will take the dog back under any circumstance.

Evaluating Your Dog for Overall Fitness for Agility

Once you think you have chosen a good candidate for agility, you must consider the overall health and conformation of your prospective competitive dog. When I say "conformation," I am talking about the overall structure of the dog: how the dog's bones and muscles fit together. I am not talking about conformation in the show dog sense, that is, how a dog conforms to the particular breed standard. The texture and color of the dog's coat, the shape of its head or ears, or overall size contributes almost nothing to whether the dog is conformed properly for athletic events. The dog's angulation, movement, and structure does.

What may be a correct conformation for the show ring may not be the optimal conformation for athletic events. Dogs that are over-angulated or

under-angulated may have shoulder or hip problems or may not move correctly. Out at the elbows, cow hocks, and pigeon-toed are all serious faults that will affect your dog's movement.

Evaluating an Agility Conformation

The way to evaluate a dog is to first study the conformation while the dog is standing and then while the dog is moving. When looking at this list, be aware that these are only guidelines. Many dogs will not or cannot conform to this due to their breed standard and overall build. For example, Bassets and Corgies will be unable to conform due to their breed standard, but there have been several successful dogs in agility in these breeds. Therefore, do not be disheartened if your dog has structural inadequacies. This does not mean he cannot do agility. In fact, many dogs are successful in spite of their overall conformation.

Have someone "free stack" your dog to examine for conformation flaws.

Examination While Standing

Show people like to "stack" their dogs before a judge, but this kind of stacking can hide many conformational flaws. It is better to "free stack" or have someone hold a tidbit out to the dog while you look at the dog in the front, back, and sides.

Overall Front: The dog's front feet should be facing forward. Shoulders should be well-angulated, forearms long and powerful. The shoulder should be approximately 30 degrees from the point of shoulder. Chest should be egg-shaped (a tapered oval) rather than barrel-chested. The elbows should rest flat against the chest. The dog should not be "out at the elbows" nor should they pinch in to create a splayed effect. Pasterns should be strong, neither straight nor down in the pasterns. Feet should be arched and compact, not splayed footed. Hare feet provide the greatest speed and jumping ability but do poorly in endurance. Cat feet, where the toes are all compacted and arched, are good for endurance but may slow the dog down. A compromise is the oval foot that is in-between the hare foot and cat foot.

Back and Chest: The back should be straight and in proportion to the rest of the body. The dog should not be roach-backed or sway-backed. A little longer back is better than too short of a back. The back should slope slightly from withers to rump. Avoid over-angulation due to stylized attempts at meeting a breed standard. (Many German Shepherd Dogs exhibit this.) Elbows should lie flat against the chest wall. Chest should be deep for full expansion, but not so deep as to interfere with movement.

Rear: Tail set should be low. Hips powerful and well-angulated, having a 30-degree

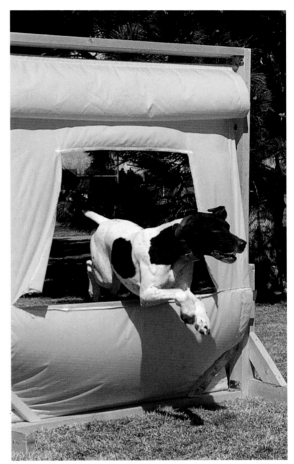

A good agility conformation enables a dog to jump effortlessly.

slope from a line drawn parallel to the ground from the top of the pelvis. Thigh should be longer to hock than from hock to toes. From the side view, the hock should have a good angulation, neither straight in the back, nor overly bent, as with sickle hocks. When looking from the rear, the hocks should be straight—neither cow-hocked nor splay-hocked. Pasterns should not be too long nor short. The rear feet should not be splayed or broken down.

Dog Gaits

Dogs have a variety of gaits. Most dogs have the walk, trot, pace, and gallop. Some dogs, such as the Greyhound, have what is called a "double-suspension" gallop, where the dog becomes airborne twice before repeating the gallop cycle.

Walk: The most energy conservative of the gaits, the walk is characterized by a slow movement. The dog will move as follows: Right-front, Left-rear, Left-front, Right-rear.

Pace: When pacing, the dog will swing two of its legs off the ground along one side and the other two remain on the ground in a Right-front, Right-rear (together) and then Left-front, Left-rear (together). This ungainly gait causes the dog to look like it is swinging its rear back and forth. Dogs typically pace when tired or lazy and wish to conserve energy.

Many conformation judges consider pacing a conformation flaw, but it is not. All dogs pace if tired. Some dogs will pace if brought into a trot incorrectly. Dogs that pace instead of trotting may have some underlying problem that may be detected by trotting the dog and observing the gait.

Trot: The trot is the most efficient gait. The dog moves by moving the diagonal legs forward at the same time. So, the movement looks like: Left-front, Right-rear in the air (moving forward) and Right-front, Left-rear on the ground; then, Right-front, Left-rear in the air (moving forward) and Left-front, Right-rear on the ground.

Because the trot is so visually precise, once you are used to seeing a good gait, you can easily detect a faulty gait or lameness that you might have trouble seeing with a walk, pace, or gallop.

Gallop: The gallop is the fastest of all the dog gaits. It may be single suspension or double suspension, depending on the breed of dog. Most dogs have a single suspension gallop where the dog is completely airborne only once in the cycle. The dog is supported by the following feet in this order: Right-front, Left-front, airborne, Right-rear, Left-rear. The double suspension gallop, which is seen in sighthounds, such as the Greyhound and Whippet, follows the order of supporting feet: Left-rear, Right-rear, airborne, Right-front, Left-front, airborne.

Examination While Moving

The best way to determine if a dog has a structural problem is to have someone gait him and watch him as he moves. To do this, you must first be able to visually watch a dog in trot and be able to distinguish abnormalities in movement. For a novice, this can be bewildering—all dogs look the same when running.

The best way to see a dog gait is to have someone trot a dog in a circle. Stand so that you can get a good view of the dog from the front, rear, and sides. If the dog is trotted correctly, you should be able to see flaws in the gait. However, someone who does not know how to trot a dog can make it appear a dog has faults when it has none. Have a friend who has done some conformation showing gait the dog if you are unsure as to what you are seeing.

As your dog trots around, you should be looking for jerky or unusual movement. Some dogs with bad gaits will crab (move sideways), paddle (swing the front feet out in a canoe paddling motion), flap (whip the foot up in a flapping motion), knit (where the hocks move up and down in a repeti-

Walk.

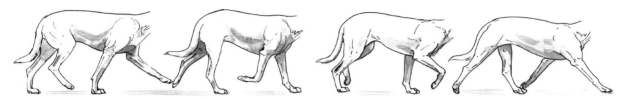

Trot.

Gallop.

tive motion), and exhibit other unusual flaws. When you first start looking at your dog's movement, watch for anything that looks jerky or ungainly.

Other Important Factors in Choosing a Dog for Agility

There are other important factors in choosing a dog for agility besides breed and conformation. These are the overall health and weight of the dog, its age, its temperament, and its training.

Health

Your future agile dog should be in good health, have all his vaccinations, and be free from internal parasites. Furthermore, Ace should be free from hip dysplasia, *osteochondrosis dissecans* (OCD), elbow dysplasia, and any other hereditary or congenital bone or joint disease. If Ace is an older dog, he should be free from severely crippling arthritis. (Some forms of arthritis may be mitigated through the use of natural supplements and medications. Talk to your veterinarian about such treatments for more information.)

Your veterinarian can easily check Ace's hips and elbows with radiographs normally used for OFA (Orthopedic Foundation for Animals) certifications. If you want an official rating or if Ace is a purebred you intend to breed later, have your veterinarian send the radiographs and a fee to OFA for an official evaluation. These ratings will become an official record with a number verifying the condition of Ace's hips and elbows. OFA does not give official ratings until the dog is two years old or older, so if Ace is young, you may have to wait for an official OFA evaluation or settle for a preliminary exam or rating.

Other health factors can affect a dog's performance. Allergies can not only make a dog miserable, but can also cause soreness due to skin and joint irritation. Tick-borne diseases such as Lyme disease and ehrlichiosis can be fatal if left untreated and will cause lameness and fatigue. Even if your dog has never had a tick on it, have your veterinarian run a blood test to determine if your dog has any of these diseases.

Lastly, blind, deaf, and unsound dogs cannot participate in agility trials. The Canine Eye Registry Foundation (CERF) provides a pass/fail rating for dogs.

If you are planning on purchasing a dog from a breeder, request to see its parents' hips, elbows, and eye certifications.

Weight

Your dog should not be overweight. Overweight dogs are slow and injury-prone. Like being overweight in humans, obesity in dogs is unhealthy. If Ace is overweight, he is at a much higher risk of developing weight-associated diseases. Jumping is more difficult and causes more stress on joints when a dog is overweight.

Most pet dogs are obese. Too often, their owners dole out their love in too much dog food, treats, and snacks. The average sedentary pet seldom needs the amount of food for an active or working dog. Many own-

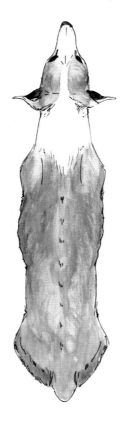

Ace should be trim and fit. The left dog is too fat, the middle dog is just right, and the right dog is too thin.

ers feed high calorie performance foods and fail to cut back the rations.

Although weighing your dog provides a good baseline when comparing it to the breed standard, it does not provide a good measure for a dog's fitness. Body structure varies from dog to dog, even within a breed, so weight should only be used as a guideline.

The best way to determine your dog's fitness is to put your thumbs on the dog's spine and feel the ribs with your outstretched fingers. You should be able to feel your dog's spine, ribs, and ribcage easily. Moving your hands toward the tail, you should also be able to feel the pelvis. If you cannot feel the spine, ribs, or pelvis, or must search to feel them (that is, they are heavily padded), your dog is too fat for agility. Consult your veterinarian. He or she may recommend a special low calorie diet. If your dog is currently doing agility, you may wish to keep your dog on a premium performance dog food, but just feed him less.

Age

There is no upper age limit for dogs to compete in agility trials as long as they are sound and not deaf or blind. Agility organizations have minimum age requirements to prevent overstressing puppies' bones and joints, which can lead to a permanent injury.

NADAC has a Veteran's class similar to the now defunct USDAA Veteran's class (USDAA Veteran's class has subsequently been replaced by the USDAA Performance Class). AKC and UKC do not have Veteran's classes, but their classes tend to be less severe than USDAA and NADAC.

How old should your dog be to optimally run agility? It depends largely on the dog. If you wish to have many years of trialing, a young dog has its obvious advantages. However, don't discount the older dog. Older dogs are frequently more mature and you may find an older dog more settled and less prone to puppy silliness.

Temperament

Obviously, a dog that is eager to please will be easier to train than a dog with an independent spirit. Australian Shepherds, Border Collies, Golden Retrievers, German Shepherd Dogs, and Labrador Retrievers generally have an intense desire to please, combined with excellent trainability. Dogs that can do tricks can also be excellent in agility.

Independent dogs such as northern breeds (those that came from Spitz-type lines) can enjoy agility, but they are much harder to train and obtain consistent performance. If your heart is set on training a northern breed, go ahead, but be warned. You need a vast amount of patience and an excellent sense of humor. Hopefully, you will be able to see past the competition and enjoy the experience. Don't be surprised if these independent dogs think up new ways each time to thwart a clean run. Kiana has surprised me with various tricks at agility trials, some never to be repeated again. One trial weekend, she walked across the broad jump boards; another weekend, she refused all contact obstacles. These incidents never occurred before in training and never occurred afterward—it simply happened. You can't train to prevent these odd occurrences, unless your dog simply isn't trained for agility and needs practice.

Any dog, with any temperament, can do agility, provided it is not aggressive. Dogs

17

TIP: Don't Free Feed

Avoid possible obesity and dominance problems by feeding your dog on a schedule. When you control the amount of food he eats, you can prevent overeating. Furthermore, your dog will look to you for his food and associate you with your care giving.

that are shy or insecure start gaining confidence as they learn to master each of the obstacles. Many owners remark on the transformation: the dog enjoys the practice and it becomes something the dog wants to do. The dog begins to show more self-confidence. Bad behaviors start to diminish. You have found a positive way to channel all that destructive energy into something positive.

Training

Dogs that are in agility usually need no formal obedience training but should be able to reliably perform a sit, down, stay, and come when called. Eventually, Ace will have to learn off-leash work. Formal obedience helps considerably since it will have already taught your dog how to come, stay, heel, sit, and down.

If you are starting with a puppy or a dog that does not know commands, enroll in a beginning or novice obedience course. Ask your veterinarian or other dog owners who compete in agility for references for good trainers who teach positive reinforcement training methods. Most good trainers are not cheap, but they have an excellent reputation and get good results. Many reputable trainers also train agility, so you may find an excellent obedience and agility instructor. If you can, find a trainer who is familiar with training your breed. Finding a trainer who has trained dogs such as northern breeds, some hounds, and other difficult dogs becomes essential if you own such a breed. If you choose a trainer who does not understand your breed, the trainer might ask you to use methods that won't work on your dog.

Don't waste your money on bargain trainers—they are usually worth less than they charge. They are often less of a bargain and more of a waste of time and money. If you purchased your agile dog or puppy from a reputable breeder, ask the breeder. Usually she can tell you where to find a good trainer in your area.

Chapter 3

Health and Nutrition

Nutrition

The Correct Diet

Just as you and I would never think to train and run a marathon on a chocolate chip cookie diet, your dog cannot perform optimally without good nutrition. If you have not already switched your dog to a premium, high performance dog food, consider doing so now. It may take six weeks or more of an acclimatization period before the dog food can actually do some good.

I say *premium* dog food because many bargain brands claim to offer the same nutrition. These bargain brands are often no bargain because they contain artificial colors, flavors, and fillers your dog doesn't need. You must often feed more of the low quality dog food to provide the same calories as a premium dog food and still not obtain the same nutrition. Dog foods that offer high digestibility figures are most likely to have useable protein sources.

The key to any dog food is the protein and fat source. Choose a dog food with the protein source as the first ingredient, but keep an eye on the next several ingredients. If the dog food lists several grain

sources such as rice, wheat, corn, and then another cheaper protein source such as corn gluten, bone meal, or soy, these ingredients may outweigh the main protein source and may actually make it into a cheaper dog food.

Whichever premium brand of food you choose, it should state that it meets the guidelines as set forth by the AAFCO committee. AAFCO is the Association of American Feed Control Officials. AAFCO has established guidelines for dogs' and puppies' nutritional needs. Most major dog food companies comply with AAFCO regulations, but you should check regardless of the brand or manufacturer.

Choose a dog food with a meat source such as chicken or poultry, beef, lamb, turkey, or by-products. By-products, depending on the ingredients, can actually be a better source of nutrition than meat. We don't like to think of our civilized canines chowing down on lungs, liver, heart, intestines, and other organ meats, but that is precisely what wolves, the ancestor of our dogs, do. When a wolf kills an animal, it doesn't just dine on the muscle meat—it eats the organs, smaller bones, hair, feathers, and fur.

Depending on what percentage of activity your dog has, you will want a minimum of a 26 percent protein and 15 percent fat by weight ratio. If your dog is chronically underweight, extremely active, or is constantly developing muscle tears and sprains and is not overweight, consider switching to a 30 percent protein, 20 percent fat ratio dog food.

Avoid vegetarian and fad diets. Vegetarian diets may be healthy for humans, but they are not good for dogs. Dogs evolved as carnivores and process vegetable protein poorly. Most vegetarian diets for dogs are low in protein and fat—the exact opposite of what an athletic dog needs! These diets use soy as the main protein source. Soy can cause gastric problems and bloating in some dogs, especially if they are allergic to it. Fad diets that have unusual ingredients or are completely natural with little or no preservatives should be at best used cautiously. These foods may go rancid quickly or may not be completely balanced.

What about home-cooked diets? Dog food has made significant advances in nutrition within the past 20 years due to intensive research. The culmination of that research appears in a bag of premium pet food. Unless you are a canine nutritionist or have done extensive research into canine nutrition, it is highly unlikely that anything you could put together would be balanced or provide all the necessary nutrients for your dog. Dog food undergoes extensive testing to be certain of the quality and the nutritional content of the food.

If you do decide to cook your own dog food, consult with a veterinarian who has experience in developing homemade diets. You should consult with a veterinary school for a feed analysis to determine protein, fat, carbohydrate content plus vitamins and minerals. Certain minerals, such as calcium, have

An Airedale Terrier completes the tunnel in competition.

specific ratios with other minerals. Too little calcium when measured against phosphorus can lead to hairline fractures and severe bone loss (as seen in an all-meat diet). Too much calcium can inhibit absorption of other essential vitamins and minerals.

Protein and Fat Versus Carbohydrates

Dogs are remarkable animals. Current studies with sled dogs suggest that dogs perform optimally on a high fat, high protein diet. Unlike human athletes, who require high amounts of complex carbohydrates, dogs require fats for energy. While training and racing, sled dogs obtain as much as 45 percent to 65 percent of their total calories in fat. Sled dogs, the top canine athletes, require 35 to 45 percent of their calories to be protein and 10 to 20 percent of their calories as carbohydrates. These dogs have been shown to do quite well with a low carbohydrate or even a zero carbohydrate diet. However, for the sake of colon health and muscle glycogen repletion, a dog should have fiber and carbohydrates. (Dogs that were on a zero carbohydrate diet did exhibit forms of stress diarrhea.)

Protein is a vital nutrient for the athletic dog. Research indicates kidney disease is not caused by high protein diets—if so, thousands of sled dogs would have kidney problems where there are none. The kidneys process excessive protein, so if your dog is sedentary or if it has kidney problems, it might be best to limit protein. (Although recent studies may suggest that dogs with kidney problems may benefit from a higher protein than originally thought.)

In a study at Cornell University[1], sled dogs incurred injuries when fed a low protein/high carbohydrate diet. At the end of

> **TIP: Table Scraps**
>
> *Table scraps are high in salt, fat, and carbohydrates and if fed frequently will actually cause an imbalance in Sierra's diet. Table scraps will make Sierra into a picky eater.*
>
> *If you must give Sierra table scraps, use them as a training treat or feed them after Sierra has eaten her normal food. Limit table scraps to less than 5 percent of Sierra's normal diet.*

the training, dogs that were fed a high protein (where 32 percent or more of the calories were protein) diet sustained no injuries, whereas every dog that was fed a low protein (16 percent of the calories) diet sustained some sort of injury. Likewise, the dogs were able to use more energy and have a higher rate of oxygen intake and carbon dioxide output when their dietary fat was significantly increased. Dogs fed diets with 40 percent of their calories coming from protein had a significantly higher plasma volume than those fed lower protein diets. Dogs that were fed high carbohydrate diets did not have the same benefits.

Dogs burn fat more efficiently than carbohydrates. According to that same report, in another study[1] at Cornell University, dogs were tested aerobically and anaerobically. One test group was fed a high fat diet and another group was fed a high carbohydrate diet. The dogs fed a higher fat diet had a significantly higher amount of free fatty acids than dogs fed carbohydrates. (Free fatty acids are used for energy by the muscle.) Further tests showed dogs perform optimally on higher fat diets than lower fat diets. Too much fat, however, is

An Alaskan Malamute performs the open tunnel.

not a good idea, as your dog can quickly become obese if not exercised. A dog should have no more than 65 percent of his calories from fat.

Unless your dog is training for a marathon each day, a premium 30 percent protein and 20 percent fat by-weight diet is very adequate. The percentages listed on dog foods are actually the percentage of protein and fat by weight—not a percentage of calories—so you must convert those by-weight percentages to a percentage of total calories to get an accurate figure. See Calorie Conversions on how to convert the by-weight percentages into total calories. The figure you come up with will be different from the ME or metabolized energy fig-

ure, which is the actual number of calories the dog can use once it is processed through the dog's system.

A good book to have on hand is *The Dry Dog Food Reference* by Howard D. Coffman. Coffman's self-published book provides an excellent reference for ingredients and percentage of protein, fat, water, and other ingredients on a dry matter or by-weight basis. With this book, you can compare dog foods and determine which performance blend is best for your dog without having to go to a pet supply store to compare. You can also obtain hard to find metabolizable energy statistics in this book—a real bonus for those who are trying to determine a product's overall digestibility.

Carbohydrates and Glycogen Replacement

Carbohydrates, however, do have their place. Dogs that perform a large amount of anaerobic activity (sprinting, jumping, and other activities that require short bursts of energy or speed) deplete glycogen within the cells quickly. Glycogen is the food a muscle cell has on hand to burn when it is called to work hard anaerobically. Those cellular reserves become depleted rapidly during the activity. For a short time after (within no more than 20 minutes after the activity), these muscle cells are receptive to glycogen repletion. By offering a simple carbohydrate in the form of maltodextrin, a glucose polymer, mixed with water or lean meat, the dog can quickly replete and maintain a higher glycogen level than a dog that does not.

There are several good commercial glycogen replacement supplements on the market including Glycocharge, Impact, and Polycose. Hydrolyzed cornstarch, available through feed stores, can provide a low-cost glucose polymer. Either DE-12 or DE-15 will work. The rule is 1 gram per pound of body weight or about 2 ounces for a 50 lb. dog. Do not use fructose-based sports drinks made for humans as they can send a dog into insulin shock. If you do feed it, give it in water, mixed with a little lean broth. (Do not mix the glycogen replacement with fat—fat tends to hinder absorption.) You must feed the glucose polymer

A Basset Hound performs the teeter.

TIP: Aerobic Versus Anaerobic

Aerobic activity is any activity that requires sustained activity and oxygen intake. In humans, this would include jogging, bicycling, and cross-country skiing. Anaerobic activity is a muscular activity that requires bursts of speed and the muscles do not require oxygen. This includes human activities such as weight lifting, racquetball, and sprinting.

Agility is an anaerobic activity. It requires anaerobic energy to jump, sprint, and climb. Dogs that frequently train for agility competition (more than three days a week) may benefit from a high fat, high protein diet.

within twenty minutes after the dog has completed exercising.

Stress Diarrhea and Diet

"Stress diarrhea" is a catchall phrase for diarrhea that appears during exercise. While it can be due to viruses and bacteria, some stress diarrhea is caused by the dog's diet. One type of stress diarrhea is from a no-carbohydrate diet due to lack of bulk in the intestines. Another type of stress diarrhea is due to too much carbohydrates and bulk. Dogs that eat lower quality dog foods may have watery, and sometimes even bloody, diarrhea due to the dog food's abrasiveness in the intestine, called rectal or capillary bleeding. A normal, healthy dog may exhibit bloody stools without any other signs of illness. This is a sign of intense training. You will most likely see this if the dog is worked every day for an hour or longer.

If Sierra has severe or bloody diarrhea, take her to your veterinarian immediately, regardless of whether you think this is stress induced. Many serious and fatal diseases, including parvovirus and distemper, can cause bloody diarrhea. If Sierra checks out normal, consider changing her diet and perhaps her training regiment to reduce this condition.

Dogs that have stress diarrhea due to high bulk or rough cut grains may benefit from switching to a high quality, highly digestible dog food. Soak the dog food to facilitate evacuation. Add a premium canned or frozen dog food that is complete and balanced. Canned dog food is usually less stressful on the intestines and makes the food very palatable.

Mushers use raw meat to combat stress diarrhea, but there are many problems associated with feeding raw meat. First, if you do not handle the meat properly, it can spoil or become a source of salmonella or other harmful bacteria. Secondly, it can be a source of parasites, depending on the meat. Lastly, meat alone is not balanced. You can cause severe calcium deficiencies because meat has high phosphorus levels. If you choose to feed raw meat, try feeding a prepared blend that is nutritionally balanced. It's more expensive than purchasing meat alone, but once you mix in the vitamins and minerals necessary to balance it with dog food, it may cost the same or actually be more expensive.

Water

Water is the most important nutrient for your dog. Your dog cannot live long without it. Every major system throughout the body uses water. Sierra cannot perform optimally if she is dehydrated. Even mild dehydration can severely affect performance, so it is very important that Sierra gets enough water.

Always provide water from a known good source. Streams and creeks may contain giardia or other organisms that may cause severe diarrhea and vomiting.

Dehydration can occur at any time of the year. During the hot summer months, a dog will drink water, but dehydration can also occur in the winter months, especially if the air is cold and dry. Some dogs may not drink enough water and may have to be coaxed into drinking. You can coax Sierra to drink by flavoring the water with bits of dog food, meat scraps, or beef broth.

Supplements

Supplements are a tricky subject, because they encompass anything given to enhance performance or nutrition in some way. Moderate supplementation can prove beneficial to dogs, but excessive amounts or the wrong supplement can have severe negative effects or even toxicity. Consult your veterinarian before you begin supplementing. If your veterinarian is not familiar with nutrition for canine athletes, contact a veterinary medical college and speak with a canine nutritionist there or ask for a referral. Many sled dog veterinarians understand the canine athlete and nutrition and are quite approachable. Consult a veterinarian or canine nutritionist for doses.

Common Supplements
· Omega-3 fatty acids—such as those found in fish oils, are excellent for reducing inflammation and may have some effect on certain types of tumors. These are

Training a Samoyed puppy on the sway bridge.

found in canola oil, flax seed oil, and cold water fish oil. Supplementing with these oils can be tricky as too much can cause hemorrhaging and severe bruising. Give no more than 5 percent of total fat calories in diet or feed a premium dog food that already has Omega-3's in it. (These dog foods frequently contain fish meal.)
· Glycogen replacers—such as Glycocharge. These are relatively new on the scene. Sled dog racers are currently using them to replete glycogen stores.
· Perna canaliculus mussel—such as Glyco-Flex. Used for joint health and arthritis. I have used this with good results, although results may vary from excellent to no difference.

- Creatine monohydrate—such as Creatcarb, SynoviCrea. Used to help build muscle. Again, this may provide mixed results.
- Glucosamine—such as SynoviCrea. Used for joint health and arthritis. I've used this with perna canaliculus mussel with good results, but again, results vary widely.
- Vitamin C—used for bone and immune system. This is a controversial supplement because dogs produce vitamin C in their bodies and have no apparent requirements for supplementation. However, many people do supplement with vitamin C.
- Vitamin E—used for muscle and heart health. Vitamin E has been a big topic in canine sports medicine since early 1999. Dogs that died of canine rhabdomyolysis ("tying-up") were found to be deficient in vitamin E. A good source of vitamin E is wheat germ oil. Vitamin E can be extremely toxic in high amounts so be certain to consult with a veterinarian or canine nutritionist for proper doses.
- Zinc—good for skin and coat health as well as the immune system. Some northern breeds (Huskies, Malamutes) have a hereditary zinc malabsorption problems that manifest themselves in the form of scaly, flaky skin along the top of the nose and muzzle, around the eyes, and on the pads. Your veterinarian must perform a biopsy to determine zinc dermatitis as opposed to some other condition such as pemphigus.
- Calcium—is used for healthy bones and joints. Puppies, dogs that are fed meat, and pregnant and lactating bitches require more calcium that adult dogs. Most dogs obtain a balanced amount of calcium through a premium dog food. Pregnant and lactating bitches will usually get enough calcium through a premium puppy food. Supplementing calcium alone is usually inadvisable as it can lead to other mineral absorption problems. Consult a veterinarian before supplementing with calcium. There are some balanced vitamins with calcium supplements that can add calcium without causing too much of an imbalance.
- Iron (such as Canine Red Cell)—is necessary to prevent anemia; however, it is easy to overdose. Talk to your veterinarian to determine if your dog requires iron supplementation. (Most do not if fed a balanced diet.)
- Bach Flower Remedies (Rescue Remedy)—this is not a supplementation, per se, but is given to dogs to calm them down or to handle stress. Because they contain no drugs, they can be given at any time without affecting performance. There are no side effects, although many conventional veterinarians may question the effectiveness.
- Homeopathic and Holistic Remedies—again, these are not necessary supplements. Most are intended to alleviate problems. Because the amount of medicine is small or come from flowers, most holistic medicines are not recognized as true medicines.

Conditioning Your Dog

Most dogs condition themselves as they start working an agility course; however, you can condition Sierra with the following activities:

- If Sierra is a large dog, you can hook her up to a bicycle attachment (such as a Springer) and do some roadwork. Be care-

A Border Collie exiting the weave poles.

ful that you start slow and run less than 1 mile the first several times.
- fetch or flying disc
- long walks
- jogging

Health Problems and the Agile Dog

Injuries and Other Conditions

Dogs can suffer a variety of injuries due to agility training. Jumping is especially strenuous on a dog's joints. A simple slip can cause an ACL (Anterior Cruciate Ligament) tear. When training and performing agility, work in a safe environment. Here are some tips:

- Jump at heights less than the dog's normal jump height for any practice except run-throughs.
- Train with nonslip and padded surfaces if you can.
- Avoid training on wet grass or slippery surfaces.
- Always warm up your dog before run-throughs.
- Train on flat surfaces with some give (dirt and grass).

Carpal Injuries: Dogs can easily injure their carpals or wrists through the repetitive pounding of jumping. This can lead to painful stress fractures and other types of injuries. If Sierra's wrists swell up after training, consider massaging them with a liniment approved for animals, icing, and then sweat wrapping them. Sweat wraps, similar to those made for horses, can greatly bring down the inflammation. Fill a plastic bag

Follow these precautions to ensure a safe workout:

- *Start with a mile or less and don't go full speed. Slowly build up the mileage. Don't overstress your dog.*
- *If you ride, walk, or jog on concrete or asphalt, consider using booties to protect sensitive pads. (You can obtain cordura booties from an outfitter that sells dog backpacks or mushing equipment.)*
- *If Sierra is panting heavily or is having trouble keeping up, slow down or rest.*
- *Be certain to give Sierra enough water to prevent dehydration.*
- *Don't exercise when it is too hot.*
- *Always talk to your veterinarian regarding any exercise program for your dog.*
- *Know the signs of heat exhaustion, heat stroke, and dehydration (covered in Health Problems and the Agile Dog).*

with crushed ice and apply it directly to Sierra's carpals. If Sierra is a thin-coated breed, first wrap a thin washcloth around the ice pack to prevent possible frostbite injury. After icing the injury for 30 minutes to an hour, remove the ice and sweat wrap the leg, being certain to cover the foot and carpals up past the carpal joint. Do not wrap too tightly or you will cut off circulation. Leave the sweat wraps on for an hour or until swelling subsides. You can alternate sweat wraps and ice. Anti-inflammatories such as buffered aspirin may help with swelling and pain. Consult with your veterinarian concerning proper dosage.

If Sierra's wrists are chronically swelling, bruised, exceedingly painful or hot, or if you suspect a fracture, seek veterinary attention. See a veterinarian immediately if Sierra is unable to put weight on the leg or is in great pain.

Shoulder Injuries: Shoulder injuries do best with massage and rest. Massage the shoulder with a liniment approved for animals and then ice. Fill a plastic bag with crushed ice and apply it directly to Sierra's shoulder. If Sierra is a thin-coated breed, first wrap a thin washcloth around the ice pack to prevent possible frostbite injury. After icing the injury for 30 minutes to an hour, remove the ice and massage again. Anti-inflammatories such as buffered aspirin may help with swelling and pain. Consult with your veterinarian concerning proper dosage.

If Sierra's shoulder is chronically swelling, bruised, exceedingly painful or hot, or if you suspect a fracture, seek veterinary attention. See a veterinarian immediately if Sierra is unable to put weight on the leg or is in great pain.

Other Impact Injuries: Depending on where the injury is and how severe, you may need to massage and rest. Massage the area with a liniment approved for animals and then ice. Fill a plastic bag with crushed ice and apply it directly to the injury site. If Sierra is a thin-coated breed, first wrap a thin washcloth around the ice pack to prevent possible frostbite injury. After icing the injury for 30 minutes to an hour, remove the ice and massage again. Anti-inflammatories such as buffered aspirin may help with swelling and pain. Consult with your veterinarian concerning proper dosage.

If the injury is chronically swelling, bruised, exceedingly painful or hot, or if you suspect a fracture, seek veterinary attention. See a veterinarian immediately if Sierra is unable to stand or is in great pain.

Dehydration and Heat Stroke: Signs of dehydration and heat stroke: elevated temperature, extreme thirst, watery diarrhea, vomiting, lethargy, high temperature (over 103°F), skin around muzzle or neck that does not snap back when pinched, difficulty breathing, weakness, and pale gums. Note: Dehydration can occur during any season and may show up as weakness, extreme thirst, and failure for the skin to snap back around the muzzle or neck.

Do not muzzle. Move Sierra into shade or cool and well-ventilated area. Give her cool water or unflavored pediatric electrolyte to drink. Soak dog in tepid or cool water. Do not use ice cold water as it will cause the capillaries to contract and not dissipate heat. Make certain the dog can breathe—remove constricting collars or other items. Obtain immediate veterinary attention.

Never leave Sierra in the car during warm weather, even with the windows down. On sunny days, the inside of a car can soar to lethal temperatures in a matter of minutes. Tinted windows and proper ventilation can help keep a car's, van's, or SUV's temperatures lower, but do not rely on that. Likewise, a dog can suffer heat stroke if left in a crate in the hot sun.

Prevent heat stroke by keeping Sierra in well-ventilated areas with shade in the summertime. Always provide fresh water. Stay out of the sun if possible.

Dog Bite Injuries: Dog bites can cause severe puncture wounds. Many puncture wounds take a few minutes to appear, so check your dog over several times if she was in a dog fight and appears uninjured. If the wounds are not serious, wash them out with a mild 10 percent betadine/90 percent water mixture. Your veterinarian will want to see Sierra and prescribe antibiotics to reduce the risk of abscesses. Check with the owner of the dog that bit Sierra to make sure its rabies vaccinations are current.

Kennel Cough (Infectious Tracheobronchitis): Kennel cough is caused by different viruses and bacteria, most notably the *Bordetella bronchiseptica* bacteria, canine adenovirus types 1 and 2, and the parainfluenza virus. Breeders and veterinarians often refer to infectious tracheobronchitis as kennel cough because it rapidly spreads through breeding and boarding kennels. Kennel cough is more of a nuisance than a serious danger to healthy adult dogs; however, it can be damaging to dogs that are very old, young, or in poor health. However, if Sierra contracts kennel cough, she will be unable to train or go to a trial for as long as six weeks. Kennel cough is highly contagious and will spread in close quarters such as boarding kennels and animal shelters. It spreads rapidly at dog shows and trials. Dogs with kennel cough have a pronounced dry cough, which may linger for as long as two to three weeks. Complete recovery may take up to six weeks. The incubation period is between five to ten days. Vaccinations against kennel cough are given once or twice yearly to adult dogs. These vaccines do not protect against all possible kennel cough viruses. Because Sierra will be exposed to many dogs from different parts of the country, kennel cough vaccinations are a good investment. The intranasal vaccine is usually the most effective.

Diarrhea and Vomiting: Changes in diet, overeating, strange water, and nervousness can cause diarrhea but so can parvovirus, internal parasites, rancid food, allergies, and other serious ailments. If Sierra is dehydrated, has a fever (over 102°F), or has extreme or bloody diarrhea, bring her to your veterinarian as soon as possible.

If your dog has mild diarrhea (soft stools—not liquid and without mucus) and does not have dehydration and is not vomiting, you can give her a tablespoon of a Kaolin product (e.g., Kaopectate) or a Bismuth Subsalicylate product (e.g., Pepto Bismol). Withhold Sierra's next meal to see if the diarrhea improves. Encourage Sierra to drink water or an unflavored pediatric electrolyte solution. If there is no diarrhea or vomiting, you can feed a mixture of boiled hamburger and rice at Sierra's next meal. If Sierra's condition does not improve or becomes worse, contact your veterinarian.

Stress diarrhea may be bloody or liquid with mucus. The dog will show no other symptoms. The dog will not need to defecate as often as a dog with true diarrhea caused by a viral or bacterial component. If you have been working Sierra especially hard lately and she begins experiencing runny stools, she may have stress diarrhea. Regardless of whether you think the diarrhea is stress diarrhea or not, take Sierra to the veterinarian as it could be something more severe such as parvovirus or distemper. Should Sierra check out OK, and if the diarrhea disappears after Sierra has stopped exercising for a few days, then you can be relatively certain Sierra had stress diarrhea.

The most common cause of stress diarrhea is diet. Mix water in with Sierra's food and let it soak. Mix canned meat-based food into her food to help provide a higher digestibility. The blood often seen with stress diarrhea is due to the rough cut grains irritating the dog's bowels.

Dogs vomit for a variety of reasons. Dogs will sometimes eat grass and vomit. Dogs also vomit due to obstructions, enlarged esophagus, parvovirus and other serious illnesses, allergies, and rancid food. If Sierra vomits more than once or twice, projectile vomits, starts becoming dehydrated, has severe diarrhea along with vomiting, has a fever (over 102°F), or retches without vomiting, bring her to the veterinarian immediately.

Foreign Objects in Feet and Other Areas (Foxtails): Check Sierra's feet often, especially if she has been outside. Dogs seem to attract foreign objects in their feet, like foxtails. Foxtails, or grass awns, are very dangerous. They have a barbed point at one end that penetrates the skin easily and can burrow itself inside a dog with each movement the dog makes. If left untreated, foxtails can become infected and cause severe abscesses.

Inspect Sierra's feet often, especially between the toes and in the spaces between the pads. Use your fingers to feel for foreign bodies. If Sierra is not entered in conformation shows, you may want to trim excess hair and feathering around the feet and legs. If you see any swollen, red skin, or feel a bump that shouldn't be there, take Sierra to the veterinarian to have it examined. (Certain cancerous tumors may also appear in the digit area.)

If you find a foxtail or other small foreign object partially buried in the skin, use a pair of tweezers to remove the object. Trim all hair around the site and then clean it with a solution of 10 percent betadine/90 percent

A good diet will help make your dog into a top competitor.

water. Apply a triple antibiotic ointment or nitrofurizone to the wound and watch for any signs of infection, redness, or swelling. Your veterinarian may have to clean the wound again and administer antibiotics.

If the object embedded is large or if Sierra is limping or in pain, seek veterinary attention.

Tick-borne Diseases

Ticks carry numerous, potentially fatal diseases such as Rocky Mountain Spotted Fever, Lyme disease, and ehrlichiosis. If you find a tick on Sierra, wear disposable latex gloves and do not handle the tick to avoid contamination. Use a good tick insecticide approved for use on dogs and treat the tick and area around it. After a few minutes, you can try to remove the tick. Use tweezers to grasp the tick close to the skin and pull out slowly. If the tick's head or legs do not retract, do not pull the tick off. The tick bite can become severely infected if you leave

the head or legs in the skin. Wait for the tick to drop off and dispose of it.

Tick-borne diseases can be insidious. If your dog shows chronic lameness, lethargy, or low-grade fever, request that your veterinarian perform a blood panel to diagnose tick-borne diseases, even if you have never seen a tick on your dog. Some diseases such as Lyme can be transmitted through nearly invisible tick nymphs.

Rocky Mountain Spotted Fever is a rickettsial organism transmitted to dogs and humans through ticks. Symptoms in the dog may include lethargy, fever, loss of appetite, diarrhea, coughing, nosebleeds, depression, lameness, and pain in joints. Some dogs may show hemorrhaging around the mucous membranes and may have blood in urine. If there is central nervous system involvement, the dog could have seizures or convulsions. Your veterinarian may treat your dog with antibiotics, usually with tetracycline. Dogs that are treated within the early stages have a good prognosis for a complete recovery.

Ehrlichiosis is another rickettsial organism transmitted to dogs, and rarely to humans, through the brown dog tick. Symptoms may include intermittent fever, lethargy, loss of appetite, and lack of stamina. Ehrlichiosis can be either acute or chronic. In the chronic stage, the white blood cells increase dramatically and may infiltrate the other organs. Dogs with chronic ehrlichiosis may show depression, hemorrhaging, nosebleeds, extreme loss of weight, loss of appetite, blood in urine, dark stools (from blood), pneumonia, and staggering. Your veterinarian may prescribe tetracycline and doxycycline. Severely ill dogs may need hospitalization and blood transfusions.

Lyme disease is caused by the bacteria *Borrelia burgdorferi* transmitted to dogs and humans through deer ticks. Lameness, fever, loss of appetite, loss of weight, and fatigue are the common symptoms of Lyme disease. Lyme may be chronic. Dogs with Lyme disease respond well to a variety of antibiotics, including tetracycline, ampicillin, and amoxicillin.

You can contract both Lyme disease and Rocky Mountain Spotted Fever from the ticks on your dog, so do not handle any ticks with your bare hands. Always use disposable latex gloves and throw them out when done. Sterilize tweezers with isopropyl alcohol.

Checking Your Dog for Lameness

You can perform your own orthopedic exam on your dog to determine if she has any injuries or soreness. The trick to doing an orthopedic exam is to go slowly and to never force the dog to move in a particular direction. If you perform the exam fast or if you force your dog to bend in an incorrect way, you can severely injure or even kill her, so always work slowly and stop with any resistance. If you are unsure how to perform this exam, if your dog is frightened or scared of being examined, or if you have a miniature or toy breed, ask your veterinarian to show you the correct way to examine your dog.

Neck

You will want to stand over Sierra, straddling her, facing forward. Gently place your right hand on Sierra's right cheek and gently push her head to the left side, parallel to the floor. (Don't let her bend her head down or up—keep it parallel.) Allow her head to go to the full range of motion until it stops in its natural

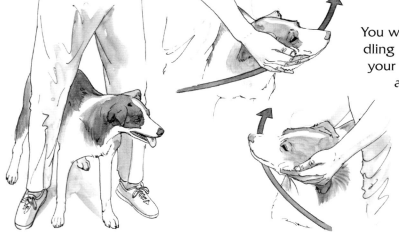

Straddle Sierra to examine her neck and front half. Gently move her head slowly from one side to the other.

Move Sierra's legs slowly through their full range of motion.

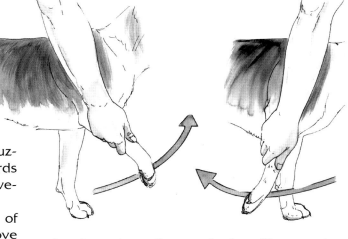

stopping point. Now, do the same thing to the right with the left hand on the left cheek. Again, do not force it.

Next, gently cup your hand under Sierra's chin and raise her head up slowly. Then gently hold her muzzle and bring her head downward towards her chest. Again, don't force the movement.

What you are looking for is any sign of distress or pain. If Sierra doesn't move through the full range of motion, *don't* try to get her to do that. Note which side is causing problems and have your veterinarian thoroughly examine her.

Front Legs and Shoulders

First, feel down each leg and inspect each paw for worn pads, broken toenails, or foreign objects. Straddling the dog, facing forward, take one leg and carefully extend it forward and then slowly move it towards the back in an arch, keeping the leg extended. This movement should follow the dog's normal movement. Do not force the dog's leg. Next, allow the leg to retract and gently take the foreleg and contract it upward towards the body as though the dog was folding it underneath her while lying down. While doing this, put your

With your left hand, slide your hand beneath the rib cage for support and with your right hand press gently on the spine in a light bouncing motion from the withers to the base of the tail.

hand on top of your dog's withers and press against the same side as the leg to push down on the shoulder while you bring up the leg. Again, do this gently.

Listen for popping or crackling sounds in the joints or if your dog shows pain or discomfort.

Back

Turn around on your dog so that you are straddling her backwards. With your left

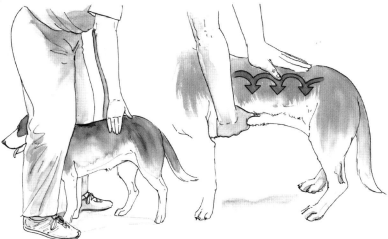

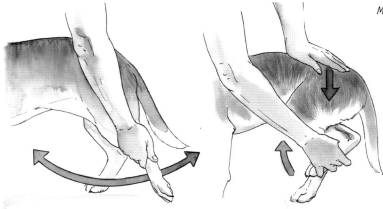

Move the leg in the normal range of motion. Then, retract the leg and press upward while gently pushing down on the hip.

ward, take one leg and carefully extend it forward and then slowly move it towards the back in an arch, keeping the leg extended. This movement should follow the dog's normal movement. Do not force the dog's leg. Next, allow the leg to retract and gently take the pastern and contract it upward towards the body as though the dog was folding it underneath her while lying down. While doing this, put your hand on top of your dog's hips and press against the same side as the leg to push down on the hip while you bring up the leg. Again, do this gently.

Listen for popping or crackling sounds in the joints or if your dog shows pain or discomfort.

Hold the tail close to the base and gently move it through its range.

hand, slide your hand beneath the ribcage for support. With the right hand, starting at the withers use your palm to gently press on the dog's spine in a light bouncing motion. Allow your left hand to travel down the dog as the right hand continues the examine. Be very gentle—the pressure should be no more than what you would use to pet her. Again, you are looking for pain or discomfort.

Back Legs and Rear

Feel down each leg and inspect each paw for worn pads, broken toenails, or foreign objects. Straddling the dog, facing back-

[1]Reynolds, Arleigh J. DVM, Ph.D., *Effect of Diet on Performance,* Performance Dog Nutrition, Performance Dog Nutrition Symposium, Colorado State University, April 1995.

Chapter 4
Training

Using Positive Training Methods

In its most basic definition, positive training is where you reward the dog when it does something right and ignore the dog when it does something wrong. Agility lends itself to positive training very well because it is often its own reward. Most dogs enjoy agility, and being praised and given treats for doing something they enjoy reinforces their learning. Kiana, my own agility Alaskan Malamute, becomes very excited whenever we get to an agility course. She loves the obstacles, being off leash, and most importantly, working with me as a team.

The secret to dog training is to teach the appropriate behavior the first time. If Ace learns the correct behavior first and you never give him the chance to fail, he is less likely to perform incorrectly. The Law of Primacy states that once a student (human or otherwise) learns something (correct or not), that lesson stays with the student. If it is a correct behavior, you are further ahead. If it is incorrect, then it becomes difficult for the student (human or dog) to unlearn that behavior.

Reward your dog whenever it performs something right. You should reward frequently with treats or with a favorite toy. At first, it may seem you are handing out treats all the time. This is all right. Just be sure that you hand out *small* treats so your dog does not become too full or too fat. Use small bits of lunch meat, cheese, hot dogs, or kibble pieces from a brand of dog food you don't normally use. Break the treat up into kibble size pieces so you can give out many treats.

When your dog does something wrong, such as performing an obstacle incorrectly, you must make your dog do what you asked for until your dog does it right before giving him a treat. Let's say Ace entered the wrong end of the tunnel (a common mistake) and is waiting for a treat. Instead of giving Ace a treat, you tell him to perform the tunnel again, only this time be certain he enters the correct end. When Ace emerges, be ready with a treat and a "Good Dog!"

Do not be tempted to use old fashion training techniques in agility. These are typically negative training methods where you provide some sort of negative stimulus such as jerking the choke chain or swatting the dog. Most national and local clubs discourage any type of negative training and have rules that you cannot use slip-type or pinch-type collars. In some trials, even a negative verbal correction might lose points or disqualify you.

In agility, you are working towards a positive relationship with your dog, not an avoidance relationship, so you will be most successful with positive reinforcement. Often when a dog does something wrong in agility, the dog does not understand or has misinterpreted what you have asked it to do. To punish a dog for something it does not understand is at the very best misguided. Never punish a dog for a mistake. You need to show Ace what you want him to do.

Which brings up the subject of correction. What is a correction? I will be using the words *correct* and *correction* often throughout the text. My definition of correction is "anything that causes a dog to cease its current actions in a meaningful manner." It does not mean hit, kick, or yell at the dog. It does not mean jerk the dog and drag it around. Correction must be meaningful in some way to the dog, that is, the dog must associate its current actions with the action you've taken. The correction must also be effective, otherwise it is completely meaningless. What you are trying to do is to guide your dog into the appropriate responses given a certain set of conditions.

An example of a correction might be as follows. Suppose Ace is always jumping up on you for treats and you do not like that. Instead of allowing him to jump up, the moment Ace comes bounding towards you, you say "no, sit!" Ace sits. You give him a treat. You have just taught the appropriate behavior, substituting one action for another.

Don't be afraid that Ace will never perform in a trial without food or toys. If you consistently train with the food and toys, he will come to expect that you have them with you and that you just chose not to reward at this time. A trial takes under two minutes; if Ace is ready for the trial, he can perform two minutes without food. Most handlers give their dogs treats before they enter the ring to have the food smell on them. They will also have a "jackpot" of treats awaiting their dogs after the run-through.

Much of positive reinforcement consists of teaching only the correct behavior and not giving the dog the opportunity to fail. If Ace only learns good habits, it is unlikely you will ever have to deal with serious problems. By applying the correct motivation (food, toys, clicker), the whole process will become fun and enjoyable for both of you.

The Tools of Training

Collars

All national agility clubs ban training type collars from competitions and some local clubs do not allow them even in practice. If a dog slips and falls, the collar could catch on a piece of equipment and severely injure the dog. Most agility clubs allow flat collars without tags.

If your dog is not reliable without a slip-type collar, look for training facilities that allow you to use them at first. Eventually, you will graduate to a flat collar.

I use a flat collar without tags that I call Kiana's agility collar when Kiana is at a trial. Some handlers run their dogs naked, that is, without a collar. Either way, this requires you to have some off leash control of your dog. Many agility trials are held outdoors with very little, if any, fencing. Ace should be able to jump the fence, so if your dog does not have a solid off-leash recall, start working on it.

Positive Reinforcement Tools

Positive reinforcement aids are anything that rewards the dog. This includes food and toys, but can also include gimmicks that give jackpot rewards. One such item is a food tube—a piece of clear plastic tubing that is slit down the center and capped at both ends. You twist the tube to fill with goodies or to reward the dog. There are commercial versions of jackpot rewarding items—most obedience mail-order catalogues carry them.

Include anything that will reward your dog. That reward is often food such as biscuits, treats, hot dogs, cheese, lunch meat, or whatever your dog really loves. The reward can also be squeaky toys, tennis balls, sticks, flying discs, or whatever your dog enjoys. Not everything works. Kiana, for example, finds food tubes and other gimmicks boring, but loves treats. Food or praise has not motivated other dogs I've owned. Your job, as an owner, is to be your dog's coach and motivator. Keep trying new combinations until something works.

Keep your food and toys hidden while you practice and only give as a reward. Otherwise, you will have a dog focused on the reward and not on the training. Use food as a lure only in the beginning and only to coax a reluctant dog onto an obstacle. I've made the mistake of using treats to lure Kiana through weave poles only to find that she focused on the food and not on the weave poles.

Many use bait pouches similar to the ones the conformation people use to hold their treats. If you are never planning to compete, you can use one. Dogs are very observant and will know when you are carrying food or not if you wear a bait bag.

Wear clothing with pockets to keep the treats in, but be certain to keep your laundry away from your dog's reach or you may find your pockets chewed through.

Leashes, Tabs, and Other Devices

When you are first working your dog, you will most likely have it on a leash for control. Use only a good latigo leather leash—chain and webbed leashes are unsuitable for training. Chain leashes do not allow good control over the dog and webbed leashes will cut into your hands. Be certain that your leash is long enough or short enough so that if you drop it (when a dog goes through a tunnel, for example), the dog's feet will not catch in the loop. Eventually, you won't be holding the leash very much. Instead, you will let it drag or drape it over your dog's back, providing some reassurance that you still have control if there is an emergency. Eventually, your dog will graduate to a tab.

A tab is a shortened leash that is anywhere from six to twelve inches in length and is knotted at the end. Trainers often use tabs as the next step to off-leash work. The dog wears the tab all the time while performing the obstacles and working off leash. The tab is long enough so that the handler can grab it and control the dog, but is short enough to give the feeling of off-leash work.

Another type of leash you might find useful are thin long lines. Some are made from parachute cord and others from thin wire or fishing line. These help when you are having problems with off-leash work. Suppose Ace discovers that once he is off leash, he is now free to act up. He starts running over to the A-frame, then the tunnel, then the chute,

Teaching the down command.

and then back to the A-frame, when all he was supposed to do was jump! You can change this by hooking up his normal leash and the thin long line to his collar and then taking the normal leash off. Work Ace as you would until he starts acting up. Then you can reel him in with a *Here!* command. Ace comes (reluctantly) and you put him in a sit. Then you praise him. Problem solved.

Commands Your Dog Should Know

Your dog should have some obedience before you start training him in agility. The pause table and pause box require that you *sit* or *down* your dog for five seconds, demonstrating that you have control over your dog. Your dog should be able to come when called, especially off leash. These are

the commands your dog must learn before it can start in agility: *Watch, Come* (off-leash recall), *Sit, Down, Stay,* and *OK.* If your dog does not know these commands or isn't very good at them, you should start working your dog now.

You may notice I have not included *heel,* and other obedience commands. This is a book on agility, not on obedience. Agility does not require heeling on or off leash, nor does it require perfect sits or downs. You can use as many commands or hand signals as you like and not get penalized. This enables you to work with your dog without worrying if an extra *come* or *sit* will hurt you. It is up to the judge's discretion on whether or not you are in control of your dog. Judges are usually lenient in the amount of commands and hand signals and will not qualify (NQ) a handler and his dog only in extreme cases.

The Golden Rules of Dog Training

• Never get angry at your dog. Agility was *your* idea, not his. If you feel yourself becoming angry or frustrated at Ace— stop training. Take a time out. Play with your dog, take a walk, or read a book. Don't take your frustration out on your canine partner.
• Become a person your dog will respect. Don't yell and scream when he does something wrong. Don't wheedle and cajole him to obey a command. Corrections and praise should be swift and meaningful to the dog.
• Always reward your dog for coming to you. Never punish a dog when it runs away and then comes back or you will be punishing the dog for coming back.

- Never force a frightened dog to do something. You will most likely get bit.
- Teach your dog to pay attention to you. You can do so with food and the *watch* command.
- Before you can teach a command, you must first have your dog's attention. Always precede the command with your dog's name, such as "Ace, *come!*" Don't say, "*Come, Ace!*" Ace is likely to have not heard the command before you got his attention.
- Say the command once and don't yell. Ace is not deaf. If he is, you'd better be teaching him with hand signals instead.
- Don't repeat the command. By repeating commands, you'll be teaching Ace that he need not obey you the first time. Sometimes with the command *come,* a dog may need some extra positive encouragement. Once the dog learns the command, the command doesn't need to be repeated unless there is a long time between when the command is given and when the action needs to be performed. (More on this in later chapters.)
- Choose one command and stick with it. Don't say "Ace, *jump!*" on one jump and then "Ace, *over!*" on another jump.
- Once Ace learns commands and you have his attention, use only the agility command. So, instead of "Ace, tire!" you should say "*tire!*"
- Choose one-word commands that don't sound like each other. *Sit down* and *lie down* are perfect examples of what will confuse your dog. Use *sit* for *sit down* and *down* for *lie down.*
- Don't use *down* for *off*. *Down* should mean lie down. *Off* should mean four paws on the ground.
- Never give a command that you cannot enforce. It's not funny hearing someone say to a dog that won't listen: "Fido, *come!* Fido, *come!* Fido, *get over here!* OK, Fido, *don't come.*" This shows an obvious lack of control.
- Always enforce a command. Let's say Ace is not reliable off leash. Keep Ace on a long line until he becomes reliable. If Ace doesn't sit after you tell him to sit, make him sit. If Ace doesn't touch the contact zone of an obstacle, make Ace perform the obstacle again and make him sit on the contact zones.
- Always reward good behavior.
- Always set your dog up for success and never allow your dog to make a mistake. This is easier than it sounds. Think through what you are training Ace for and what possible responses he can have. Be prepared for them. Remember: *It is easier to teach good habits than it is to unlearn bad ones.*
- Always end a training session on a positive note.

Learning the sit *command is especially helpful on the table where the dog must perform a* sit *or* down.

- Have fun. (If neither of you are having fun, why bother?)
- Take time to play. Ace needs some play time with you to release stress and excess energy. Have fun with your dog.

Teaching Commands

The following is a brief guide to teaching basic commands. For more in-depth training, choose a good book on positive obedience training or consult a professional trainer. Initially, you should spend about ten to fifteen minutes a day working on commands. After Ace is familiar with the commands, shorten your training sessions to five to ten minutes. In this section, I'm assuming that your dog already knows most of the commands and isn't perfect with them.

Anytime that you are teaching a command and the dog becomes aggressive or fearful, stop immediately. Evaluate what you are doing to cause this behavior. Some commands, such as sit and down, require the dog to be placed in a submissive position. Some dogs don't like being touched in this fashion. These are dogs that are either highly dominant, have not been handled much, or have been smacked too often. If you own such a dog, it would be wise to consult a dog behaviorist or a professional trainer. She can show you how to properly train Ace to accept commands.

You should have trained your dog to take treats from you without losing your fingers in the process. If Ace is a piranha when you offer a treat, hold the treat in your fist and lightly rap him on the nose when he tries to grab it. Say "Nice!" and offer the treat. After a couple of raps on the nose, Ace should get the idea that he isn't going to get the treat unless he does so politely.

Watch Me

Watch or *Watch me* is a command where you reward your dog for focusing on your face. This is an easy command to teach. You can do this by cutting up cheese or hot dogs into small pieces and bringing it up to the bridge of your nose. Say, "Ace, *watch me!*" When Ace makes eye contact, give him the treat. Some trainers will actually put the pieces of food in their mouths and when the dog makes eye contact, then will give him a piece.

Come (Off-leash Recall)

If your dog is unreliable on recalls, go back to the basics and use a training collar and a six-foot leather leash. Sit your dog, if Ace will sit, otherwise leave him standing, and go out to the end of the leash. Say, "Ace, *come,*" and give a little tug on the leash. Your voice should be upbeat and happy, not authoritative or angry. If Ace does not come, reel him in with gentle encouragement. Clap your hands and repeat the command. Give him a treat the moment he arrives and make a fuss over him. You may want to teach him to sit in front of you before you give him the treat.

Once Ace recalls reliably on a six-foot leash, you can start lengthening the distance. You can accomplish this by using a long line or a long retractable leash. Practice your recalls in areas such as parks that have distractions. If Ace can reliably come when called, you're both ready for the next step.

The next step involves letting your dog think he is off leash. Put a light long line on Ace with his leash so that when you take off the regular leash, you still have control, but Ace is convinced he is off leash. When you

Teaching stay *and* come.

do so, practice in a secure area, such as an indoor training facility or a fenced-in backyard. Start from only ten feet away. Gradually lengthen the distance. Once Ace proves he is reliable in a secure area, move to an unsecured area with many distractions. If you ever have to use the long line, go back to the leash and work on his on-leash recalls.

Eventually, you will want to try your recall off leash. Again, practice in a secure area. If you have been doing your on-leash recalls faithfully, the off-leash recall should go smoothly, but occasionally it doesn't. If Ace wanders or tries to run off, collect your dog, put him on a leash and start at the beginning. Don't work in an unsecured area off leash if you can help it. It only takes a moment for your dog to become distracted and bolt, and all that training is gone.

Sit

Teaching Ace to sit is relatively easy. Have Ace standing beside you. With one hand, hold a treat over his nose, just out of reach and move it backward. With the other hand, lightly push down on his rump and say "Ace, *sit!*" Give Ace the treat when his rump touches the floor. Practice *sit* often and always reward Ace when he performs correctly.

Down

Down tends to be a little more difficult to learn than *sit*. Put Ace in a sitting position and hold a treat at level with his nose. With a swift movement, bring the treat to the ground closer to Ace's chest and say "Ace, *down!*" Ace will hopefully try to follow the

Stay

Put Ace on a leash and put him in *sit* or *down*. Tell Ace "Ace, *stay!*" and move your outstretched palm in a sweeping motion towards his face. Take one or two steps and turn around. If Ace tries to follow you, say "No, Ace, *stay!*" and move Ace back into his original position. Don't scold or act angry. You don't want Ace to break the *stay* because he is apprehensive.

Ace will eventually stay for a nanosecond. Before he gets up, give him a treat and quietly praise him "Good *stay*, good Ace!" If he gets up, put him back in his place. Wait a few seconds and if he stays, give him a treat again. Give him another treat before releasing him. Release him after he stays for ten seconds. Continue working with him staying for only ten seconds a few feet away until he has mastered it. Eventually, increase the time to twenty seconds. Give Ace treats while he is maintaining his stay. You will eventually increase dis-

Teach sit *by holding a treat over Ace's nose and move it backward while lightly pushing down on Ace's rump. Say, "Ace, sit!"*

treat and drop to the ground. If he needs help to complete the *down*, you may lightly push on his shoulders. Give Ace the treat only when he is in the proper down position.

Never use the word *down* when you mean *off*. Otherwise, Ace may get confused when you put him on the pause table and tell him *down*. He may jump off because you've been telling him *down* when you meant, "get off the couch!"

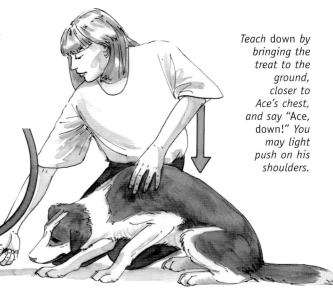

Teach down *by bringing the treat to the ground, closer to Ace's chest, and say "Ace, down!" You may light push on his shoulders.*

Teaching stay.

tance and time, but do not increase both simultaneously.

You may be able to guess when Ace will break the *stay* and be able to give him a treat before he breaks his *stay*. Anytime Ace shows nervousness or breaks his stays frequently, drop down to a shorter distance and a shorter time so he can have a successful *stay*. Remember: set your dog up to succeed.

OK

OK is the release word you will use whenever you put your dog in a sit, down, or stay. Ace will pick up on OK quickly because he knows this will release him from whatever you've made him do. OK is a good command to let your dog know he's completed the agility course and a good release word for when he is to break his *stay* or continue to the next obstacle after resting on the contact zones.

Commands Your Dog Needs to Learn

Your dog needs to learn a few extra commands to work agility courses. Luckily, these commands are closely related to obedience commands, and your dog should learn them easily.

Here

Here is similar to *Come* in many respects. Many agility handlers use *come* instead, but I prefer *here* to differentiate the situation. *Come* is often used in obedience for coming directly to the handler and sitting perfectly—something you don't necessarily want in agility! Start your dog loose in a secured area and say, "Ace, *here!*" and show him the treat. Ace should come running for his treat. Reward him with the treat and lavish praise. Don't make him sit or correct him if he leaves again.

The purpose of *here* is to bring your dog closer to you to guide him to an obstacle. Sometimes the difference between taking the right obstacle or a trap depends on your ability to bring your dog a little closer to you.

I use *here* as a game with Kiana. She will run around off leash for a while and then I will call her *Here!* She always comes running because she knows I have a treat ready.

Get Out!

Get out! is the opposite of *here!* If Ace loves to play fetch, *Get out!* is an easy command to teach. Throw the ball and tell Ace *Get out!* when he chases after the ball. You can then tell him, *Here!,* and reward him when he brings the ball to you.

Even if Ace isn't a fetching type of dog, you can still teach *Get out!* Toss biscuits in different places away from you and use the command *Get out!* whenever he goes to retrieve them. He automatically gets his reward, the biscuit, for heading out.

Rest or Wait

Rest or *Wait* is similar to *stay* in many ways, except it is only a brief pause on the contact zones on obstacles. Even if you don't have contact zones you can still teach *wait* or *rest*. As you walk your dog, say *wait* and hesitate for a moment. You can put him into a sitting position with a treat if he does not pause long enough. Continue walking and surprise him with *wait* occasionally.

Take Time to Play

Throughout training, it is very important to take time to play with your dog. Obedience and agility training is very demanding, no matter how enjoyable it might seem. End every training session positively with a game your dog enjoys, whether it's fetch, flying disc, or tag. Ace will look forward to training sessions more often if they are positive and fun.

Chapter 5

Puppy Training

Choosing the Puppy

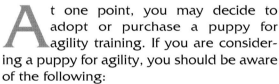

At one point, you may decide to adopt or purchase a puppy for agility training. If you are considering a puppy for agility, you should be aware of the following:

- A puppy will not be ready to compete until it is one to two years old. Many agility organizations have age restrictions.
- Be prepared to keep the puppy even if she does not become the agility competitor you had hoped for. Hereditary and congenital diseases such as hip dysplasia, OCD, and elbow dysplasia may end a puppy's agility career. The puppy may not be fast or agile enough to obtain high placements.
- Raising a puppy is time-consuming and expensive.
- Puppies require extensive socialization and training.

If you are determined to own a puppy and start her in agility, choose a puppy you will love to have as an adult dog, no matter how long or short her agility career is. To purchase a puppy only for the sake of High in Trials and then to sell or give her away because she cannot perform is irresponsible at best. Not only do you add to the number of unwanted pets, but you also have taken a home away from a shelter or rescue dog. Choose a breed that is compatible with your lifestyle and personality. If you live in an apartment or townhouse, a toy breed may suit your requirements. If you are active and looking for a dog that will join you in the outdoors, consider a working breed. Different breeds have different temperaments as well. *The Encyclopedia of Dog Breeds,* by D. Caroline Coile (Barron's), provides an extensive overview of the breeds and their characteristics. Once you have chosen a few possible breeds, contact the breed clubs through the AKC and obtain information concerning their breed. The national breed club can usually refer you to local breeders in your area who would be happy to talk with you concerning their breed and its characteristics.

Where to Find Your Puppy

Always purchase a puppy from a reputable breeder. You can obtain a list of breeders in good standing with the breed club by contacting the AKC directly and requesting contact information for the national breed club. Most breed clubs have breeder referrals or can direct you toward the local breed club in your area. Many national breed clubs

**TIP: Pet Quality
Versus Show Quality**

If you are looking for a pure-bred and you are not interested in showing in AKC conformation shows, consider obtaining a pet quality puppy. Unless there is something physically unsound with the puppy, a pet quality puppy can be a bargain agility competitor.

Having your puppy explore new things prepares him for agility.

have breed rescues—an excellent place for obtaining older dogs and puppies. Don't discount rescue—many agility gems came from rescue as diamonds in the rough.

Study the breed carefully, not only for agility aptitude, but also for temperament and hereditary diseases. Some diseases, such as hip dysplasia and progressive retinal atrophy (PRA), are in all breeds, but there may be certain hereditary diseases specific to the breed you are considering. For example, some lines of Dalmatians and Australian Shepherds may carry deafness. Alaskan Malamutes have a crippling dwarfism called chondrodysplasia. Some Dobermans, Rottweilers, and Weimaraners have Von Willebrand's Disease (VWD), a type of hemophilia. Yorkshire Terriers can have liver shunts. A reputable breeder will screen for not only hip dysplasia and eye diseases, but also for breed specific diseases. Ask for certifications. If the breeder is unable to provide you at least with the certifications from the Orthopedic Foundation for Animals (OFA) and the Canine Eye Registration Foundation (CERF) for both parents, consider looking elsewhere. Verbal promises such as "he's had his hips checked," will be soon forgotten if your puppy has hip dysplasia. Be certain that your breeder's contract guarantees that your puppy is free from these genetic diseases and that the breeder will offer money or a replacement if a veterinarian diagnoses your puppy with one of them.

Choose a puppy from working, obedience, or agility lines. If the parents have agility, working, or obedience titles, chances are your puppy will have some aptitude for agility. This is no guarantee, of course, because many fine competitive dogs have come from unknown or questionable backgrounds and even the finest purebreds have produced duds. Still, you are more likely to have a puppy with better aptitude if the puppy's ancestors are out of working stock.

Request to see the breeder's contract before looking at puppies. If the breeder is reputable, he will guarantee the puppy's health and that the puppy is free from hereditary defects. Many reputable breeders will have caveats concerning working the puppy before a certain age—jumping and other stressful work may cause joint problems. However, the breeder should not have restrictions in the guarantee that are impossible to meet. Such clauses might include extreme restrictions on exercise or diets that are nearly impossible to meet.

Every reputable breeder will have a clause of "Right of First Refusal" or "First Right of Refusal" stating that you will notify the breeder if you no longer want the dog. Furthermore, the breeder should have a statement saying that he will take back the dog, if you no longer want the dog or can no longer care for it. The breeder should also have a spay or neuter clause if the puppy is pet quality.

Tell the breeder what you intend to do with the puppy and ask for recommendations as to which puppy you should choose. The breeder often knows the puppies' temperaments and can make suggestions. Your puppy should be no younger than eight weeks of age. Do not take a puppy younger than this because the puppy needs this time to socialize with her mother and littermates.

If you choose to adopt a mixed-breed puppy or a purebred puppy from rescue, you risk the unknown parentage and unknown treatment. Despite these drawbacks, many rescue dogs prove to be good in agility competition with time and patient

training. Mixed breeds can have genetic diseases such as hip dysplasia, elbow dysplasia, or Progressive Retinal Atrophy (PRA), an eye disease.

Choosing a Puppy from a Litter

A good agility puppy is outgoing, not shy or timid (although many shy or timid puppies have changed due to efforts of their handlers). When it's time to select your puppy, you should find a puppy that is not overly dominant or submissive—both can cause problems for the novice agility trainer. Your puppy should show interest in you, but be willing to explore. Roll or bounce a ball near the puppies. They should show interest in the ball, not fear or submission. With permission of the breeder, gently roll the puppy on her back while on the floor and hold her there gently while rubbing her tummy. Overly dominant puppies will struggle vigorously and may try to snap or bite. Let go of the puppy if she struggles fiercely or becomes upset. A submissive puppy will lie there without any struggle. A normal puppy will struggle a little and then relax as you rub her tummy.

Clap your hands, whistle, and cheerfully call to the puppy while she is looking away from you. She should react to the noise in some fashion—the best reaction should be that she should come to you happily. If she ignores you, it could be a sign of deafness or being extremely independent.

Take the puppy to your veterinarian for a thorough exam before you bring her home. Your veterinarian will wish to check your

This puppy is learning how fun agility can be.

TIP: At What Age Can They Jump?

Puppies have what are called "growth plates" in their legs. These bone plates are not fused together as they are in adult dogs. Until these growth plates come together, there is a potential for severely injuring your puppy through jumping and strenuous work. Since different breeds grow at different rates and there are variations within individuals, you should ask your veterinarian when it will be safe for your puppy to jump.

You can, however, have the puppy become familiar with jumps and their attached wings. Set the jump height lower than your puppy's hock joint and lead her over.

puppy's overall health. If your puppy is of unknown parentage or is older, your veterinarian may suggest a hip X ray to determine if her hips are sound. Again, tell your veterinarian that you have purchased this puppy for agility training and discuss any concerns. Your veterinarian may want to vaccinate your puppy if the puppy is due for her vaccinations. Follow your veterinarian's advice concerning vaccinations.

Limited Registration Versus Full Registration

The AKC has two forms of purebred registration for puppies of known pedigree: limited registration (with purple stripes running across the document) and full registration (printed normally). A dog with limited registration cannot compete in conformation shows nor can it have its pups registered through the AKC; however, it does not affect your dog's ability to obtain agility titles. Every pet quality dog should be spayed or neutered before it reaches six months old.

Another type of registration is the ILP (Indefinite Listing Privilege) in AKC and the LP (Limited Privilege) in UKC. Both serve to provide the ability for dogs of unknown pedigree that are obviously purebred to be registered to compete in their respective trials. Both AKC and UKC require photographs and proof of spay or neuter. This registration is typically done for shelter and rescue dogs. Dogs with an ILP or LP cannot compete in conformation shows, but can compete in other events such as obedience and agility.

Early Basic Training: Two to Four Months

From the time you bring Sierra home and up until she has had all her vaccinations (about sixteen weeks old), your main focus should be on teaching her that all good things come from you. You should also be training good habits that will last the rest of her life. While socialization is very important for Sierra, you should refrain from exposing her to strange dogs until she has had all her vaccinations. Parvovirus and distemper are two deadly diseases that can kill her. Parvovirus is transmitted through fecal matter and may live in soil for up to one year. Distemper can be transmitted through the air and you can accidentally carry the disease on your clothing or shoes.

Begin teaching Sierra the following:
- Coming when called. Always have a treat or biscuit on you to reward Sierra when she comes to you.
- Defecate and urinate on command. (A useful command to use before entering the trial ring). Use the words "go potty!" or "hurry up!" when Sierra eliminates. Praise her after she has relieved herself.
- Crate training. Feed and give treats in her travel crate. Put her travel crate and bed in your bedroom and have her sleep there.
- Enjoying car rides. Take your puppy to fun places while in the car once she has had all her vaccinations. Drive her to a park for a walk, to a friend's house to play with his or her dog, or to a fast food drive-through for a snack.
- Basic commands: *sit, lie down, come,* and *stay.* All training should be positive reinforcement training.

- Teaching confidence over unusual surfaces. Try walking your puppy over portions of an exercise pen (x-pen) laid flat or through a ladder lying on the ground.

Puppies enjoy going through tunnels as much as children.

Early Agility Training: Two to Six Months

Although Sierra is very young, you can still play games with her and lead her over obstacles that will prepare her for agility later. Use the following obstacles and games:

- Puppy in a Blanket—Use an old towel or blanket for this game. Begin with a treat hidden in your hand under the blanket or towel. Coax Sierra to nose under the blanket and reward her with a treat. You can continue playing this game by coaxing her farther under the blanket. Encourage her to find her way out, but never allow her to get tangled or frightened by it. (Preliminary closed tunnel training.)
- Walk the plank—Put a 12-inch (30 cm) wide by 10-foot (3 m) long plank on top of two cinder blocks. Lure Sierra onto the plank using food and teach her to walk across it. (Preliminary dogwalk and crossover training.)
- Walk the ladder—Walk Sierra through the ladder rungs while the ladder is lying on the ground. (Teaches footing.)
- Tip the board—Cut a piece of 1½ inch (4 cm) PVC pipe to about 2 feet (60 cm) long and then cut it in half so that you have a half circle of pipe. Cut a piece of plywood to about 18 inches by 24 inches (46 cm × 60 cm). (It can be longer or shorter.) Lure Sierra onto the board with food and slowly teach her to tip the board. You can actually show her where the tip point is here.
- Through the tunnel—Purchase a child's tunnel or use the fixed portion of a chute to create a straight tunnel for Sierra to go through.
- Early weaves—Begin with stick in the ground type of weave poles. Put them in a wide pattern as when you first teach weave poles for an adult. Teach Sierra to run through the columns as you would with weave pole training (see Chapter 12).

Early Training: Four to Six Months

Once Sierra has all her vaccinations, she should be protected enough for you to enroll her into a Puppy KPT class or Puppy Kindergarten class. In Puppy Kindergarten class, she will be able to socialize with puppies her own age and safely explore new surroundings.

Puppy on tippy board.

Wait until your veterinarian gives his approval before jumping Sierra. A puppy's growth plates should fuse before taking obstacles.

Bring Sierra on longer car trips. Trips can be to the pet supply store, to public parks (on leash), and to fun matches to get used to crowds and large numbers of dogs. If you do take Sierra to a place with other dogs, be certain to keep her under control. Do not allow her to come up to any other dog without the owner's permission. Many dogs, even those who are well trained, poorly tolerate puppies and strange dogs. To avoid causing a fight, keep your puppy with you and never allow her to invade the space of another dog.

After Puppy Kindergarten, enroll Sierra in a novice obedience class. Many dogs benefit from obedience training as it teaches the puppy how to learn. Choose an obedience trainer that uses mostly positive reinforcement methods.

Continue to work on the socialization and commands from the two to four months section, plus add the following commands:
· *Sit*
· *Down*
· *Stay*

TIP: Training Young Puppies

Young puppies have a shorter attention span and tire more easily than an adolescent or adult dog. Keep training sessions short (five to ten minutes) and fun. Use lots of treats and positive reinforcement. If Sierra becomes tired, stop. Most puppies will not know their limits and will actually play beyond their energy reserve.

- *Heel*
- *The Heel Position*
- *Come*
- *Here*
- *Get Out*
- *Go Right*
- *Go Left*

- AKC—twelve months
- NADAC—eighteen months
- UKC—six months
- USDAA—eighteen months

Agility Training: Six to Twelve Months

At this stage, you can start introducing the obstacles to Sierra in their training configurations. Keep the A-frame in a lower and less severe configuration to avoid stressing joints and be certain to keep jumps below hock level. Use extra caution when your puppy is on the dog walk, crossover, tower, or teeter. A fall from these obstacles can severely injure or kill a young puppy. Likewise, use care on the chute—a puppy can become terrified from one incident of being tangled in the chute.

In Summary

You can train good habits and good behavior at an early age that will prepare your puppy for agility competition for the rest of her life. In order to do this, you must do the following:

- Establish yourself as someone fun to do things with (someone your puppy wants to be around and wants to listen to).
- Socialize your puppy with people and other dogs.
- Acclimate your puppy to new situations. (Instill confidence.)
- Teach your puppy to travel well.
- Teach your puppy to learn.

Chapter

6

Finding the Right Club or Training Class

Choosing the Style That's Right for You

A t the time of this writing, there are four major national agility organizations or sanctioning bodies: AKC, NADAC, UKC, and USDAA. You can participate in all or one, depending on what you are looking for in agility. If Sierra is a mixed breed, she is limited to NADAC, UKC, and USDAA trials.

Depending on your area, you may be further limited by availability of classes and trials. Most areas have either AKC or USDAA trials.

If you have a fast dog, consider USDAA or NADAC. Perhaps you are more interested in control rather than speed. UKC focuses on handling rather than top speed. AKC is a nice combination of the two for purebreds.

Remember that competition is not about winning. It should be fun for you and your dog.

Both NADAC and USDAA offer classes or divisions for the Junior Handler.

The National Clubs

AKC

AKC Agility is sanctioned by the American Kennel Club. If you have a purebred already registered with the AKC, you can sign up for any AKC events. If Sierra is a purebred that is unregistered, (i.e. has no papers), you can still register her with an ILP (Indefinite Listing Privilege) number. Sierra must

be spayed in order to qualify for an ILP. Contact the American Kennel Club for more information at either (919) 233-9767 or their website: *http://www.akc.org/*.

AKC offers two classes: standard and jumpers with weaves. In standard classes, the dog must perform on all the AKC obstacles, with the exception of the weave poles for those in Novice. In jumpers with weaves (JWW), the dog must perform a course with no contact obstacles or tables. JWW is a faster run than the standard course and is scored differently than the standard class.

AKC's trials rival those of USDAA in number, in spite of their relatively recent involvement in the sport. In 1999, the AKC had over 700 sanctioned trials. This is possibly due to the fact that the AKC is an older organization and is a breed club rather than an agility sanctioning body. Conformation and obedience kennel clubs now host agility trials as well as local agility clubs.

NADAC

NADAC, or the North American Dog Agility Council, has another form of agility. To compete in NADAC-style agility, you must register your purebred or mixed-breed dog with NADAC, but NADAC does not require your dog to be spayed or neutered. NADAC offers a faster pace than AKC, but also offers a veteran's and junior handler's division as well as a standard division. NADAC's jump heights are not as high as USDAA's. The Veteran's class, intended for older dogs or handlers, is lower. NADAC also has an exemption for certain breeds, allowing lower jump heights for larger, deep-chested breeds.

NADAC offers a standard class, which includes all NADAC obstacles, including weave poles. They also offer a gamblers and jumpers class.

Checklist for Choosing a Professional Dog Agility Trainer

- Is the trainer familiar with agility? Is the trainer familiar with the style of agility you want to train with?
- Does the trainer train you to train your dog?
- Does the trainer use positive methods to train dogs?
- Does the trainer have references?
- Does the trainer own dogs with agility titles? Does the trainer compete for titles?
- Does the trainer allow you to watch a training session?
- Is the trainer gentle or harsh with dogs?
- Does the trainer's philosophy coincide with your own?
- Does the trainer have equipment that is to regulation standard?
- Does the trainer have enough room for run-throughs or at least sequencing?
- Does the trainer work on sequencing and not just obstacle training?
- Does the trainer have a regimented class or is it a drop-in type class?

Agility training class—if you are just starting out, look for a regimented class first.

UKC

UKC, or the United Kennel Club, has a form of agility based on the NCDA (National Club for Dog Agility) rules. UKC allows purebreds and mixed breeds, if registered with UKC. Mixed breeds must be spayed or neutered. The courses are shorter and times are slower; emphasis is placed on handling, not on overall speed.

In UKC, novice dogs may compete in AG-I or AG-II classes. AG-I has contact obstacles, jumps, a table, pipe tunnels, and chutes. AG-II has crawl tunnels, pause boxes, platform jumps, weave poles, sway bridges, jumps, and swing planks. Both courses look very different from each other. AG-II is a faster course.

In UKC trials, emphasis is placed on correct entries and exits and the handler not breaking the "plane of the obstacle." This means that the handler can't hover over the obstacle or put his or her hand over the obstacle. Likewise, the handler is not allowed to recall the dog or block obstacles.

USDAA

The oldest and most established of the national agility organizations in the United States, USDAA, or the United States Dog Agility Association Inc., has perhaps the most varied classes. USDAA courses are faster paced with higher jumps than any of the other agility organizations. USDAA, like

NADAC, allows mixed breed dogs without a spay or neuter requirement.

USDAA has three programs: Championship, Performance, and Junior Handlers. Classes include standard, jumpers, gamblers, snooker, and relay. USDAA's performance program now takes the place of the veteran's class. It has lower jump heights, lower A-frame, and slower times. Anyone may compete in the USDAA performance class.

USDAA also offers the following championship tournaments: The Grand Prix of Dog Agility World Championships, the Dog Agility Masters Team Championships, and the Dog Agility Steeplechase Championships.

Other Agility Sanctioning Clubs

There are other agility sanctioning bodies such as ASCA (Australian Shepherd Club of America) and AAC (Agility Association of Canada) that accept all breeds.

What to Look for in a Training Class

Most agility training classes are offered through obedience trainers or training clubs. Ask your veterinarian, clubs that sponsor agility trials, or other agility handlers where there are good agility instructors. Once you obtain a list, visit those instructors while they are teaching a class. You should visit the training session without your dog to determine if you like and approve of the class and the trainer's style of teaching.

Most trainers hold two types of agility classes. One is the regimented class where everyone in the class works on a particular object or handling technique. The other is a drop-in type class where the individual handlers work on whatever each person feels their dog needs practice with. Both types of classes have their benefit. In the first type of class, the class is regimented and the handlers learn a specific technique or obstacle from the trainer. They get more attention and more focus than they would if they were all training individually. This method is good for beginners and those who need to learn new handling techniques. The downside of this training is if you and your dog need practice on another obstacle or another technique, you must work on what the class is working on.

The drop-in type class is good for those who need to practice certain techniques that they've already learned or to work on an obstacle that the dog is having problems with. While beginners can learn new obstacles in this environment, it may be more difficult than learning in a regimented class setting. The trainer or trainers may be helping someone else with a piece of equipment while you are trying to teach Sierra the teeter and may need help.

If you are just starting out, look for a regimented class first. You can then attend drop-in classes to work on practicing certain obstacles or new techniques you've learned. If you can, look for a variety of classes in different facilities. You can learn different training techniques and gain different insights as to how to train Sierra. Not only that, but Sierra will become comfortable with different equipment and different settings—something she will need to do if she is at a trial.

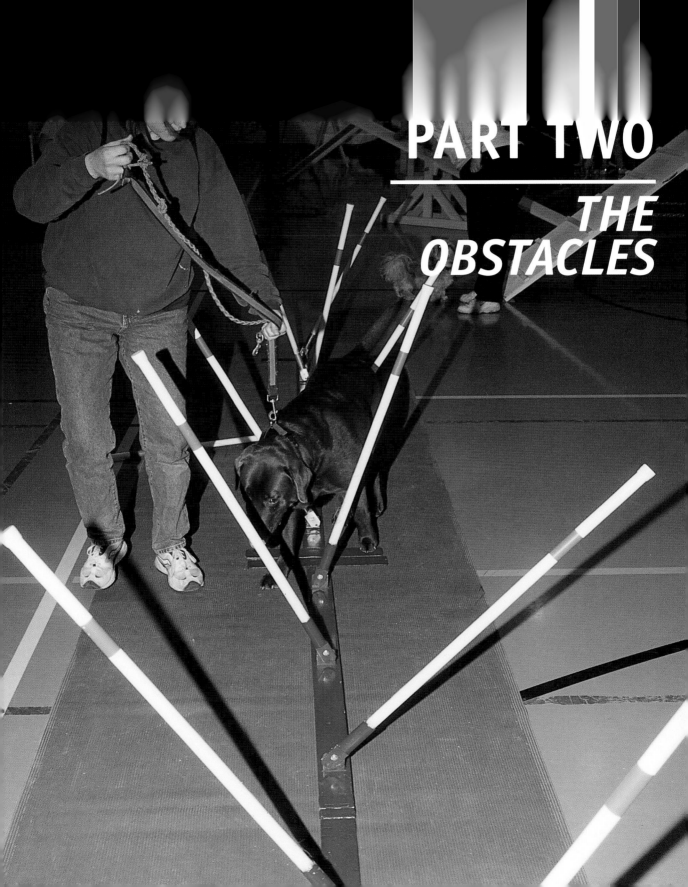

PART TWO

THE
OBSTACLES

Chapter 7

Introducing Your Dog
to the Obstacles

There are two parts to teaching your dog agility: learning obstacles, and handling and sequencing. In learning obstacles, your dog gains confidence in his ability to tackle any new set of problems. He learns to trust that you will help him negotiate the obstacle without causing injury. Some obstacles, like the teeter-totter and sway-bridge, move once the dog is on them. Other obstacles, such as the weave poles, are not intuitive to master and the dog cannot learn them without your guidance.

I cover handling and sequencing in Part Three: Putting It Together. I cannot stress enough how vital this is. Once Ace has achieved some mastery over the obstacles, the temptation exists to enter Ace into an agility trial. This is like asking a child who has just learned the alphabet to write a best-selling novel. Certainly, she has the basics, but until she learns to spell and learns the rules of grammar, she can't construct a simple sentence, let alone write anything worth merit. So too is agility. Your dog must learn not only the obstacles, but also the ability to work as a team with you. You too must learn proper handling to show your dog where you want it go and what you want it to do. Luckily, motivated dogs learn quickly and with the proper training

can become competitive within a year or two.

Likewise, the temptation exists for the owner to start Ace out with the most difficult obstacles in their primary configuration. I've seen people new to agility set jump bars too high, coerce dogs across a piece of equipment, or push them through tunnels, only to have them balk or worst yet, panic. What is intuitive for us humans is not intuitive to the dogs.

This is not entirely the owner's fault. Perhaps he is at a match or a trial and sees dogs jumping 24 or 26 inches (60 cm or 66 cm). He doesn't realize there are height divisions, so he makes his Jack Russell Terrier jump

> **TIP: Teaching Appropriate Approaches**
>
> *How your dog approaches an obstacle influences how she will perform. Sloppy approaches can lead to missed contacts, refusals, run-outs, or fly-offs. They can also be dangerous—a dog that enters an obstacle incorrectly has a greater chance at falling off than an appropriate approach. If you decide to enter Ace in a UKC trial, sloppy approaches will deduct points from your score.*

A Pomeranian performs weave poles in a training class.

8 inches (20 cm), then 12 inches (30 cm), and then goes for 16 or 20 inches (41 cm or 51 cm) in a kind of canine game of one-upmanship. Or perhaps he tries to make his Golden Retriever cross a 12-foot (3.7 m) dog walk for the first time and the dog nearly falls off. Then, discouraged, he feels that Ace will never become competitive in agility. This is furthest from the truth. Instead, the owner should realize that the beginning dog has limitations—much of them mental—when he is trying to learn the obstacles. The owner must learn to communicate with his dog and show it what he wants it to do.

Most clubs and training centers lack beginning and intermediate equipment due to cost. Likewise, there is very little novice

equipment available. Wherever possible, I will try to suggest beginning training strategies and novice equipment.

When you go to a training center, expect to keep your dog on a leash (or at least a tab) while you work with him on the obstacles. Many places do not allow training collars of any type, so check with the center before showing up with slip or prong collars.

You may notice the various specifications for each sanctioning group with each obstacle listed. Some obstacles, such as the open or pipe tunnel, may have little variation in sizes, whereas the A-frame sizes may differ greatly. The sizes are correct as of this writing; however, the sanctioning bodies may change these requirements over time. Use this only as a guideline—if you

A Great Dane pops out of the tunnel.

need the actual regulation heights, contact the appropriate sanctioning group.

All at Once or One at a Time?

So, what is the best training method to introduce your dog to the obstacles? Should you start with one, achieve some sort of mastery before going on, or start with all of them? It depends on the dog. Some dogs figure out the obstacles quickly and are ready to try another in a very short time. Other dogs have extreme difficulty learning more than one obstacle. It may be best to start with two or three obstacles that can be easily mastered and then progress to the more difficult ones.

Obstacles that are less daunting than others (if they are set in a beginning configuration) are: jumps (provided they are set low enough), pipe or open tunnels, hoop tunnels, A-frame, table, and weave poles. Later, as Ace gains confidence, you can add the dog walk, closed tunnel, teeter, and other obstacles to his repertoire.

If Ace has a bad scare on an obstacle or is tired of one obstacle, try switching to another obstacle that is less intimidating or one that he understands. This will help build his confidence when he finishes the training session with something positive.

Gaining Mastery of One or More Obstacles

Depending on the dog and the amount of training, your dog should be able to learn most obstacles in a relatively short time. However, to perform an obstacle consistently well requires many months of training.

Percy, the Yorkshire Terrier, climbs up the tower stairs.

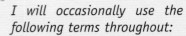

TIP: Terminology

I will occasionally use the following terms throughout:

- *Refusals—A refusal is where the dog either balks or hesitates before an obstacle or passes the plane of the obstacle.*
- *Run-outs—A run-out is where the dog runs past the obstacle, causing a refusal.*
- *Fly-offs—A fly-off occurs when a dog leaves the teeter while the end of the downward side of the teeter is still in the air.*
- *Contacts—The sections that mark the entry and exit points of the contact obstacle. They are painted in a different color, usually yellow, and are approximately 24 to 42 inches (30–107 cm) long, depending on the equipment and the sanctioning organization.*
- *Off-course—The technical term for performing an obstacle not in sequence to the actual course. A dog can perform an obstacle that is not used in the course (a dummy obstacle), that is out of sequence, or even the correct obstacle, only performed in the wrong direction.*

Chapter 8

The Contact Obstacles

Teaching Contacts

The contact obstacles are generally slower than jumps, tunnels, or weaves. To perform them, Sierra must stand on and move across them. The dog walk, the teeter-totter (or seesaw), and the A-frame are contact obstacles common to all agility organizations but you may see the crossover and tower depending on the club or sanctioning organization.

The contact obstacles can be very intimidating to some dogs. Large dogs may have difficulty negotiating the narrow planks of the dog walk and crossover, while smaller dogs may find the A-frame daunting. Many dogs have difficulty learning the seesaw because of its movement. Even so, once a dog masters the contact obstacles, they often become favorites. It's not unusual to see a large dog launch herself at an A-frame or a small dog enjoying the new height advantage of the dog walk.

Most dogs do not think about the placement of their back feet. While this sounds amusing at first, it becomes a challenge to teach a large dog the dog walk and the teeter. Large dogs will often walk up the dog walk with their front feet only and stop when the planks get too high. Assuming you do

manage to coax the dog to the highest point, the dog may stop and become fearful, shaking the obstacle. I've carried 75-pound (34-kg) dogs off the dog walk to prevent them from falling. A spill off the dog walk is a very negative experience. Kiana fell off the dog walk when we first started agility. After nearly three years of not doing agility, we started again. She remembered her fear of dog walks and we had to work through that before continuing.

One way to teach your dog to learn where its feet are is to put a 12-inch (30-cm) wide ladder on the ground and have your dog walk through it. Sierra will quickly

Start teaching your dog to pause on the downside of the contacts now to prevent nonqualifying scores in the future.

TIP: The Importance of Resting or Waiting on Contacts

Start teaching your dog to pause on the downside of the contacts now to prevent nonqualifying scores in the future. You can be severely penalized or eliminated if your dog fails to touch the contacts. The contacts are on both the up and down sides of the obstacle. They are usually yellow, in contrast to some other color the obstacle is painted.

While dogs are not completely color-blind, I have yet to see a dog that can distinguish the contact color from anything else. It is up to the handler to stop the dog at the contact. You can do so with the touch, rest, *or* wait *command.*

When Sierra starts walking down the dog walk, A-frame, or teeter, give your command touch, *offer Sierra a treat, and say "Good Dog!" It usually takes a few tries before you can get the timing right, where Sierra pauses on the obstacle's contact. After a few times, when Sierra hears the word* touch, *she will pause and wait for the treat before leaving the obstacle.*

is the least intimidating. If Sierra is small, she might do better on the dog walk.

Test all equipment before using it. Wobbly equipment at best will discourage your dog; at worst, it could collapse under her! Kiana has used her share of rickety equipment and every time she experiences it, we must then find a good piece of equipment so she can become confident again. Avoid shaky equipment if you can. Unfortunately, some end up in trials and the refusals add up fast. If you suspect a problem with the equipment, bring it to the attention of the judge immediately.

Another method of training contact obstacles is called back-chaining. Back-chaining involves physically placing your dog at the end of the obstacle and allowing her to walk off. As she gains confidence, you continue to place her further up the obstacle, until she is confident to work the entire obstacle. This method works for small and medium-sized dogs that the owner can pick up easily, but if Sierra is a Great Dane or if the owner cannot lift her because of a physical impairment, back-chaining may not be an option.

A-frame

realize that she must place her feet correctly or stumble on the rungs and sides of the ladder. This is good training for both the seesaw and the dog walk. Later, you can graduate Sierra to a plank set across concrete blocks. Both are nonthreatening.

If you have a large to medium-sized dog, you should have at least one helper when teaching your dog the contact obstacles. You will need someone capable of supporting the dog from either her front or rear end. If you have a larger dog, the A-frame

AKC

Height: 4 feet 11 inches (8-foot ramps); 5 feet 6 inches (9-foot ramps)
Ramps: 8 or 9 feet long; 35–49 inches wide.
Contact Zones: 42 inches.

NADAC

Height: 5 feet 6 inches
Ramps: 9 feet long; 3–4 feet wide.
Contact Zones: 42 inches.

The A-frame.

UKC

Height: 59 inches (8-foot ramps);
   49–50 inches (6 feet 8 inch ramps)
Ramps: 6 feet 8 inches or 8 feet; 30–48 inches wide.
Contact Zones: 40–42 inches.

USDAA

Height: 6 feet three inches (Performance Program: five feet 6 inches)
Ramps: 9 feet long; minimum 36 inches wide.
Contact Zones: 42 inches.

The A-frame is a large contact obstacle originally borrowed from Schutzhund training. It is a heavy obstacle with two 8 to 9-foot ramps that meet to a peak in the center and has a width of three to four feet. The dog must scramble to climb the structure and then climb down it, hopefully in a controlled fashion. The A-frame is one of Kiana's favorite obstacles, giving her what must seem a bird's eye view over all.

Many large and medium-sized dogs find the A-frame the easiest contact obstacle to master. Small dogs may find the A-frame daunting at first, in which case, the dog walk proves a good first obstacle. Dogs with joint and bone problems (arthritis, hip dysplasia, OCD), or weaker and overweight dogs may find the A-frame too stressful. This is why you should have your veterinarian fully examine your dog before starting agility.

If your club or training facility allows you to lower the A-frame so there is not a steep angle, do so. This will help your dog become comfortable with the object. Put a leash on Sierra's flat buckle collar and lead her over. Say "scramble," "A-frame," or another word unique to the A-frame. Pause her at the contacts with a *touch* command. Give her lots of praise and treats. Sierra is likely to wonder

1. Lower the A-frame to training height and lead your dog over it while on leash. Weazel, the Australian Cattle dog demonstrates with her owner.

2. After practicing with the lowered A-frame, bring the A-frame up to regulation height. Lure your dog up the A-frame with treats and lots of praise.

3. Lure your dog down the A-frame. Have Weazel focus on you, not the height.

4. Pause on the contacts.

what the big deal is after a few sessions of this, so slowly raise the A-frame's height a few notches and try it again. After Sierra becomes comfortable with the new height and angle, raise it again. Finally, you will be working the A-frame at its normal height.

If you do not have the opportunity to train with a lowered A-frame, you will have to train with it at normal height. This wall seems to daunt most dogs at first. Put a leash on Sierra's flat buckle collar. Take her straight on with a good approach, give

Weazel demonstrates her agility aptitude.

If Sierra is the kind of dog that balks the moment you approach the A-frame, you may have to coax her up. Bits of hot dog, liver, or some other treat combined with your enthusiastic encouragement may be enough to convince Sierra this is a fun activity. Keep Sierra focused on you and the food the first few times. Once the A-frame is no longer scary, Sierra is likely to enjoy the obstacle and you probably will have difficulty keeping her off it!

Sometimes after a dog has performed the A-frame a few times, the dog gets a little daring and once on top, may stop and look around or try to leap off it. As a handler, you should still have Sierra leashed and pointed in the direction where you want her to go—namely downward. Never allow your dog to jump from any contact obstacle—this can cause serious injury.

Depending on which agility regulations you compete under, your dog may be required to touch the upside and downside or just the downside of the A-frame's contact zones. In AKC rules, for example, the

her the command *scramble* or *A-frame,* and lead her over. Don't give Sierra a second to pause and reflect on her predicament. Dogs that linger on the top of the A-frame may be tempted to leap instead of climbing down. Your job is to keep Sierra's head pointed in the right direction. Give Sierra a treat and lots of praise.

The dog walk.

dog does not need to touch the contact on the upside, but must on the downside.

Dog Walk

AKC

Height: 36 inches (8 foot);
   48 inches (12 foot)
Ramp Length: 8 feet or 12 feet
Ramp Width: 12 inches
Contact Zones: 42 inches

NADAC

Height: 46–50 inches
Ramp Length: 12 feet
Ramp Width: 9¼–12 inches
Contact Zones: 36–42 inches

UKC

Height: 36 inches
Ramp Length: 8 feet (can be up
   to 3 inches shorter)
Ramp Width: 12 inches ± ½ inch
Contact Zones: 48 inches

USDAA

Height: 48–54 inches
Ramp Length: 12 feet
Ramp Width: 9–12 inches
Contact Zones: 36 inches

The dog walk is a tall obstacle that has two ramps joined by a long plank. The dog must walk up the ramp, traverse the plank, and walk down the opposite ramp to perform the obstacle. Small dogs usually have little difficulty, except maybe with the overall height. Larger dogs tend to have footing problems due to not thinking about their back feet. Prepare Sierra for the dog walk with a ladder or a small bridge made from a plank and cinder blocks. (See instructions earlier in chapter.)

To teach Sierra how to perform the dog walk, you will need a second person that will spot the dog on the other side and keep her from falling off the dog walk. With large dogs, both you and that person may need to guide Sierra's foot placement. Start

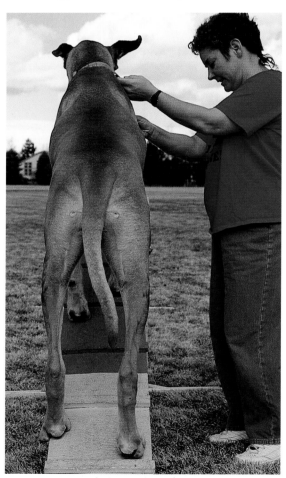

1. Larger dogs tend to have a footing problem
with the dog walk. Stetson, the Great Dane,
and his owner demonstrate.

2. Use two people to help a novice dog learn the dog walk. The second person helps guide the back feet along the narrow plank.

4. Lure Stetson down the dog walk with food. Again, have Stetson focus on you and the food rather than the height.

3. Have Stetson focus on you and the food rather than the height while luring him across.

5. Pause on the contacts. "Yes, Stetson is a big dog!"

Sierra walking up the dog walk, paying attention to where she is putting her feet. She may need some coaxing with treats. You can use them as either a lure or put them along the dog walk in a "Hansel and

Gretel" fashion. Use unique words such as *dog walk, walk it,* or *walk* as a command.

Some trainers like to line the dog walk with little tidbits to keep the dog focused on the dog walk rather than the overall height. This works as long as you do not leave treats in the middle where a nervous dog can pause and consider her predicament. Treats should be small and easy to swallow. You do not want Sierra to spend more than a second to eat the treat. Tiny bits of hot dogs, liver, pieces of soft meat, rolls (Rollover) and other like tidbits work well. Avoid rawhide pieces, biscuits, and other treats that require extensive chewing. The treats you use for luring can be placed as follows: on the edge of the contacts, halfway and three-quarters the way up and down the ramps, and a foot or two from each side of the ramps along the plank.

Once Sierra has gone beyond the length of the plank, the tendency is for her to rush down the opposite ramp. Too fast and Sierra may fly off the ramp without touching the contacts. Go slowly and give her the command to touch the contact. Physically sit her down on the contact and give her a treat. It does not take long for Sierra to pause on contacts and look expectantly for treats when you say *touch* or whatever command you use for touching contacts.

You should position yourself so that if Sierra has a misstep, you can catch her before she falls. A tumble off the dog walk can be serious or even fatal, if Sierra is small. If, for whatever reason, Sierra falls off the dog walk, check her over and make sure she is all right. Then, continue training. That's right: practice agility. You may not want to work with her on the dog walk right now, but you do want to leave her with a positive experience.

Crossover

USDAA

Height: 48–54 inches
Ramp Length: 12 feet
Ramp Width: 9–12 inches
Contact Zones: 36 inches

Think of the crossover as dog walk on steroids. It has four ramps, instead of two, on each side and meets at a small platform in the middle. With the crossover, you must add directional control as well, leading your dog to the appropriate side. Once on top, choose the path she will take to walk down. Sierra must first listen to your commands before she can master the crossover.

Sierra should be completely comfortable with the dog walk before you attempt to take her on the crossover. Train with a flat buckle collar and a short leash or tab, as you would a dog walk. You may want a second person as a spotter or handler, just in case. Motion Sierra to the side you want her to go on and choose a straight-ahead approach. Use the command *cross* or *crossover* to designate it as a different piece of equipment. Sloppy approaches will cause an incorrect entry and possible problems. Give Sierra plenty of encouragement once she commits to the obstacle. Once she reaches the top, give Sierra the pause command and give her a treat. Then show her which section you want her to walk down. Don't forget to have her touch the contacts at the end.

If Sierra is familiar with the dog walk, the crossover shouldn't be difficult. Work on different entries and exits to be sure Sierra will not choose the same ones each time. She should be looking to you for direction.

Teeter-totter

AKC

Height: 24 inches
Ramp Length: 12 feet
Ramp Width: 12 inches
Contact Zones: 42 inches

NADAC

Height: 24 inches
Ramp Length: 12 feet
Ramp Width: 9¼–12 inches
Contact Zones: 36–42 inches

UKC

Height: 16 inches (8 foot), 20 inches (10 foot), or 24 inches (12 foot)
Ramp Length: 8, 10, or 12 feet
Ramp Width: 12 inches ± ½ inch
Contact Zones: 24 inches

USDAA

Height: 24–27 inches
Ramp Length: 12 feet
Ramp Width: 9–12 inches
Contact Zones: 36 inches

The teeter-totter or seesaw is probably the most intimidating of the contact obstacles. It is, as the name suggests, a seesaw that moves up and down with your dog's weight. Most dogs find the movement unsettling and refuse to stay on what appears an unsteady object. Dogs that have a negative experience on the teeter may balk at the dog walk since the approach

TIP: Prevent Fly-Offs

A fly-off is when a dog hops off the teeter before the teeter touches the ground. Fly-offs happen for a number of reasons, but the most common causes are either the dog isn't comfortable with the teeter or the dog is moving too fast. Sometimes it is both. To prevent fly-offs, teach Sierra to stop at the pivot point and slowly tip it over and then touch the contact zones.

Besides getting you eliminated or severely penalized, fly-offs are dangerous. A dog can injure herself in the jump or when the teeter swings down. I've actually seen a fly-off when a dog hopped off the teeter, but the jump was too short and the dog landed directly on the contact patch. That is still a fly-off, since the dog's feet were not in contact with the teeter the entire time while the dog was performing the teeter.

The teeter.

1. *Lead your dog up the teeter. Cheri, the Basset Hound, and her owner demonstrate.*

looks alike. Dogs may also lose confidence in other agility obstacles. This is why I recommend, and many people leave, the teeter as one of the last obstacles to learn.

A few instructors teach the teeter first. The rationale is that once the dog learns the teeter, all the other obstacles are easy. While there is some truth to this, if you are teaching your dog yourself, you risk having a bad experience and ruining any hope of having a confident dog in agility. Leave the teeter-first training to the professionals and work on learning other obstacles before dealing with moving ones such as the teeter, the swing plank, and the sway bridge.

To teach the teeter, you need a spotter along the other side. Use a flat buckle collar and short leash or tab to guide Sierra into a straight approach. Give her the command *teeter* or *seesaw* and lead her up the plank

2. *Use a second person to hold the teeter to prevent it from tipping as the dog reaches the pivot point.*

3. Carefully lower the teeter and lead your dog down. Don't let the teeter bang.

right before the pivot point. Sierra may naturally assume that this is the dog walk and may try to forge ahead beyond the pivot point. *Do not allow her to tip the teeter by herself!* Instead, take hold of her collar with one hand and the plank in the other. Your spotter should take the plank in her hand and be ready in case Sierra tries to squirm off. Slowly move Sierra forward. Say *work it, tip it, easy* or some command that will alert Sierra she is right at the pivot point. Allow Sierra's weight to move the teeter a little, bring the end up a little, and then slowly move the plank slightly down and up until you allow it to gently touch the floor. Pause her at the contact zone before allowing her to step off. Give plenty of praise and encouragement.

4. Cheri demonstrates her aptitude on the teeter.

TIP: The Four-Paw Rule

The four-paw rule in AKC and USDAA competition means that once your dog has put all four paws on a contact obstacle and has jumped off, the dog cannot attempt the obstacle and the handler and dog must continue on. The handler cannot put her dog back on the contact obstacle or will be excused from the ring. The run will be nonqualifying.

In contrast, UKC allows three tries at any contact obstacle. So, even if your dog fails to perform an obstacle the first time, you can put her on again and still qualify!

If Sierra is like most dogs, the movement may alarm her. Perhaps she will try to wiggle free of your grasp. If she truly panics, stop the movement and let her calm down before continuing. Your praise and reassuring voice will help make it positive. Give her treats before the pivot point. Then move her forward to the pivot point and slowly move the plank until it touches the floor. More treats and praise.

After Sierra experiences the teeter once, take her to another obstacle that she is confident in and enjoys. Work her on the other obstacle for a few times and then take her back to the teeter. Repeat the process with the handler. Then work Sierra on another obstacle. Give Sierra a total of three or four practice sessions on the teeter and end with practicing obstacles she is confident with.

The next time you train, repeat the process from the first day. Your task is to have Sierra feel comfortable with the teeter. If she goes up it without encouragement, stop her before the pivot point, give her a

1. Percy, the Yorkshire Terrier, is lured up to the tower platform.

treat, tell her *work it!* and help her find the pivot point. You still need to hold the teeter to prevent it from crashing down as Sierra tips it. If Sierra is still nervous, continue to use a second handler and repeat the lessons from the first day.

As Sierra shows more confidence each time you train, you will want to give her more of a feel for the teeter. Many large dogs will stop at the pivot point and bow, almost pushing the teeter down. Some small dogs will creep to the pivot point and stand, waiting for the teeter to slowly lower itself down. Sierra will no doubt create her own technique for triggering the teeter.

Tower

None of the national agility organizations have towers, but I've seen them at local clubs, so they are worth a mention. The tower is similar to the cross-

Tower obstacle.

over because you have a choice of directions. The tower I've seen has a plank, a set of stairs, and a slide. You choose the direction your dog goes up (stairs, plank) and the method your dog comes down (slide, stairs, or plank.) The stairs and plank were relatively easy to master, but the slide was a little unusual.

Treat the tower as you would a crossover. If there is an unusual component such as a slide, use a handler to help you with your dog. You will want to slow your dog at the slide by holding her and gently sliding her down the smooth ramp. Provide lots of treats and encouragement.

Help Sierra down the slide until she becomes comfortable with it.

Use treats to lure Sierra up the stairs.

2. Percy, the Yorkshire Terrier, going down the tower slide.

Chapter 9
The Jumps

Before You Begin

Teaching Your Dog to Jump

As strange as it might seem, dogs are not born good jumpers. They have the ability to jump, but like anything learned, it must be taught. I had no idea of this when I returned to agility with Kiana—I simply assumed the Malamute could jump with precision because she had jumped hurdles before. Accurate and fast jumping requires skill and precision, something many dogs don't have.

When you start training, you should start with low jumps and work your way up. Often the novice is convinced that his dog must jump the highest possible height at the start. Many will set the bar much higher than the regulation heights in a "how high can you go?" contest. It might satisfy the owner's ego to know that his 12-inch (30 cm) high Beagle cleared a 24-inch (60 cm) jump, but this is not good agility. Nor is it healthy for their dog. Quite often, these contests only seek to hit a mark, not to hit it accurately.

When you start teaching jumps, set the jump height below Ace's hock. If Ace is a

The tire jump.

small dog, such as a Yorkshire Terrier or Chihuahua, you may want to leave the bar on the ground. Put a leash on Ace's flat collar and lead him to the jump. If the jump is winged or a spread-bar type jump, have Ace investigate it. Then carefully lead him over. Use enthusiastic encouragement and the command *Over! Jump!,* or *Hup!*

If you've set the jump low, it shouldn't take more than a quick hop to clear it. Give him treats and praise. Many larger dogs will probably walk over it without noticing. This is good—you want your dog to be confident in his approach.

Once Ace is completely confident going through the jump, put a long line or tracking lead on Ace's collar. Put him in a sit-stay and walk over to the opposite side of the jump while still holding the leash. Stand on the other side to the right or left of the jump and call him over. "Ace, here! Over!" Gentle tugs and treats in your hand should easily guide him over the jump. Practice with Ace jumping beside you or with you directing Ace to the jump from a distance.

Now, raise the bar. The bar should be the next level higher or a level where Ace needs to jump a little to get over it. Practice running Ace through at the new height until he gets used to it. Then practice directing Ace to the jump. Always use treats and praise as a reward.

Once Ace is proficient at jumping at a lower height, you can raise the bar to the

TIP: Knocked Down Bars

What do you do if Ace knocks down a bar during training? This will lead to a nonqualifying score in AKC, UKC, and USDAA Standard Class and severe faults in USDAA and NADAC. Stop what you are doing, put Ace in a sit or down-stay, and pick up the bar and replace it. Because you have suddenly stopped the fun, Ace will see something has gone on that requires a down-stay.

Sometimes a knocked-down bar is not Ace's fault. You may not have given him enough room to successfully complete the jump. Situations such as refusals and run-outs may lead you to attempt a jump without the proper room. Ace may not have the ability to short-hop a jump without knocking it down. Always be certain Ace has enough room to successfully perform a jump.

Jump Height Regulations: *These jump heights are for normal vertical jumps, not for the broad jump and the spread hurdle jumps, which will be covered in their description. These heights are current as of this writing.*

AKC

AKC Height at Withers	Jump Height
10 inches and under	8 inches
14 inches and under	12 inches
18 inches and under	16 inches
20 inches and under	22 inches
Over 22 inches	24 inches

NADAC

NADAC Height at Withers	Jump Height
11 inches and under	8 inches
13 inches and under	12 inches
17 inches and under	16 inches
20 inches and under	20 inches
Over 20 inches	24 inches

UKC

Height at Withers	Jump Height
14 inches and under (Division 1)	8 inches
20 inches and under (Division 2)	14 inches
Over 20 inches (Division 3)	20 inches

USDAA

USDAA Height at Withers	Jump Height
12 inches and under	12 inches/8 inches
16 inches and under	16 inches/12 inches
21 inches and under	22 inches/16 inches
Over 21 inches	26 inches/22 inches

You must first have your dog stand in a good posture before measuring your dog at the withers. Tape a piece of paper about the height of your dog to a nearby wall. (Use masking tape so it will not peel off the paint!) Stand your dog next to the paper and lay a flat ruler across the top of your dog's shoulders. (Also called the withers.) Mark the place where the ruler touches the paper and account for any extra thickness. Use a tape measure and measure the wall from the mark to the floor. That is your dog's height in inches.

Training at Maximum Height or Less?: *Once Ace is able to jump the required height, should you train Ace at that height all the time? Probably not. Jumping is a strenuous activity and repetitive jumping at heights such as 24 or 26 inches can cause injury.*

If you train frequently, choose a jump height below the requirements. Vary the heights to provide some challenge. However, if you are preparing for competition, set most practice run-throughs at the regulation height. You should set certain jumps, such as the tire jump or the broad jump, to maximum height or length because they are trickier to perform correctly.

A Puli jumps in agility competition.

Have a second handler stand beside to jump to prevent Ace from running around the jump and getting the treat, otherwise you will have rewarded the wrong behavior. Stand with Ace, release him, and give him the command, "Over!" Ace should jump over the hurdle and get the treat or toy on the other side. After a few sessions, when Ace learns this new game, lengthen the distance between Ace and the jump. You can also vary the approaches.

What about long jumps, such as broad jumps and spread jumps? The same training applies, only now you will be asking Ace to hurdle over longer distances. Use the lowest spread jump or one or two sections for the broad jump. Put a leash on Ace's flat collar and lead him to the jump. Use enthusiastic encouragement and the command *Over! Jump!,* or *Hup!* Some people like to use the words *Big over!* or *Big jump!* However, Ace shouldn't need this extra command to jump long.

A problem with broad jumps is that it may not look like a jump to Ace. Ace may instead

next level and practice at a new height. With each level of proficiency, increase the height until Ace is finally at the height he needs to be for competition.

To teach Ace to lead out over a jump, put Ace in a sit-stay and place a treat or favorite toy where Ace will land on the other side.

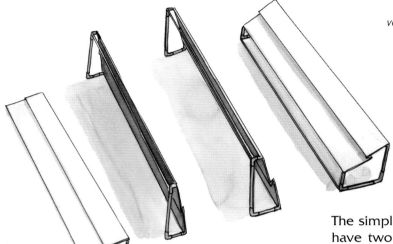

Turn a few boards on their sides to give a vertical appearance to the broad jump. Otherwise, Ace may not see the broad jump as a hurdle and he may simply walk across it.

jump. The extra height, combined with your jump command, may encourage Ace to jump rather than walk over the boards.

The Bar Jump

The simplest of all jumps, the bar jump will have two bars set crosswise between two uprights. Set the first bar at the height the dog must jump. The second bar should be set about midway between the bar and the ground. The second bar helps the dog see that this is a jump.

One bar jumps are more difficult because they do not use the second bar as a visual aid. Dogs may run through them, under

opt to walk across the boards instead of jumping over them. You can correct this easily by either turning a few broad jump boards on their sides to give them more of a vertical look or use a single bar jump on the lowest or second lowest height in front of the broad

Train your dog over low jumps first to learn how to jump properly.

Panel jump.

them, or past them or may misjudge the height. One bar jumps are seldom used in novice courses.

The Panel Jump

The panel jump is a hurdle that is made from flat plastic or wood that causes the jump to resemble a solid wall. This is similar to the high jump in obedience, except that the boards are displaceable.

Once the tire is at regulation height, Ace may not recognize it as a jump and may instead attempt to crawl under. You can stop this by putting a second jump underneath the tire, or a piece of plywood or Plexiglas to block the lower area.

The Tire Jump

AKC

Inner Diameter: 24 inches
"Tire" Width: 3–8 inches thick

NADAC

Inner Diameter: 20–24 inches
  Must be displaceable

UKC

Inner Diameter: 30 inches
"Tire" Width: minimum 3 inches thick

USDAA

Inner Diameter: 17–20 inches
"Tire" Width: minimum 4 inches thick

The tire jump, also known as the hoop or circle jump, is possibly the most technically difficult jump to master. Many dogs see the space below the tire jump, rather than the jump itself, and walk through underneath instead of jumping over. The tire jump consists of a "tire" (usually irrigation hose) and a frame made from wood or PVC. You measure the height from the bottom of the aperture to the ground. The tire jump should be adjustable in its frame using bungee, chains, or rope. You should be able to set it to the proper heights.

Start teaching the tire jump at a lower height than Ace's normal jump height. This will familiarize him with jumping through objects, not just over them. You may use a leash to train him, but quite often, the leash becomes an encumbrance rather than an aid.

Window jump.

(You must drop the leash when he jumps over the tire jump.) Use a tab or unclip the leash right before he jumps.

As Ace becomes more comfortable with the tire jump, increase its height. If Ace is in the 20, 24, or 26-inch class, train at a shorter height until he can become comfortable with the tire. Once you are able to set the tire at the regulation height, Ace may not recognize it as a tire and may run underneath instead of over. You may have to resort to using a leash or you may try blocking the space below the tire jump with a bar jump or a piece of plywood or Plexiglas. Some people wrap plastic wrap underneath to provide a barrier the dog can see through.

Use the word *tire*. Jumping through the tire is very different from jumping over a bar jump, so the word *tire* is a cue. I like to add *over!* when Kiana lines up for the tire. This is superfluous, I know, but Kiana has come to expect the command *Tire, over!* However, when you teach the tire (or the window, which is similar to the tire), try to use only one word.

The Window Jump

AKC

Aperture: 24 inches or 24-inch square
Minimum Width: 12 inches thick from aperture to frame

UKC

Aperture: 14 inches wide by 30 inches tall

The window jump could be considered an easier version of the tire jump. Like the tire jump, the window requires precision in jumping *through* the jump, rather than just over it. Unlike the tire, the panels that create the window are opaque, giving Ace only one way to perform the obstacle.

Teach the window jump in the same fashion as you would the tire. AKC uses the window jump and the tire interchangeably (you are more likely to see the tire on AKC courses), so, some people use the command *tire* for the window jump. This is fine. I use *window* because Kiana and I have trained with both the tire and the window.

Window jump. Dee Dee, the German Shorthaired Pointer, makes short work of the window jump.

The Double Bar Jump (Parallel Spread Jump)

AKC

Distance Between Center Bars

Height	Spread Between Center Bars (between center points)
8 inches	4 inches
12 inches	6 inches
16 inches	8 inches
20 inches	10 inches
24 inches	12 inches

The double bar jump consists of two parallel bars that are set apart a specified width. Like the bar jump, the top bars are set at regulation height and the lower bars are set midway for visibility. These jumps require more run-up room and more precision.

Double bar jump.

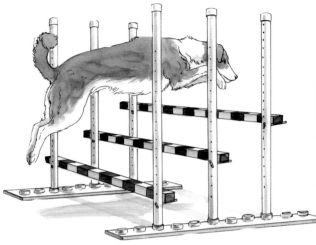

Triple bar jump.

classes. It requires more run-up distance than other jumps due to the combined overall length and height.

UKC

Jump Divisions*	Number of Bars	Height of Bars
Division 1 (8 inches)	2	4 and 8 inches respectively
Division 2 (14 inches)	3	4, 8, 14 inches respectively
Division 3 (20 inches)	4	4, 8, 14, 20 inches respectively

*Note: span between bars is 6 inches in all divisions.

USDAA

Spread	12- and 16-inch Jump Heights	22- and 26-inch Jump Heights
Regular Parallel Span	N/A	12–15 inches inclusive
Regular Ascending Span	10–12 inches	15–20 inches inclusive
Extended Span (Ascending Only)	12 inches	20–24 inches inclusive

The spread jump is similar to the AKC triple bar jumps in many respects. Like the AKC double and triple bar jumps, these jumps require longer run-up distance and more precise jumping. Spread jumps are

The Triple Bar Jump

AKC

Height	Distance Between Bars	Bar Heights
8 inches	4 inches	4, 6, 8 inches respectively
12 inches	6 inches	6, 9, 12 inches respectively
16 inches	8 inches	8, 12, 16 inches respectively
20 inches	10 inches	10, 15, 20 inches respectively
24 inches	12 inches	12, 18, 24 inches respectively

The triple bar jump is an ascending jump seen in the AKC Open and Excellent

not allowed in Performance or Junior Handler programs.

The Broad Jump

AKC

Height	Length
8 inches	16 inches
12 inches	24 inches
16 inches	32 inches
20 inches	40 inches
24 inches	48 inches

UKC

Height	Length
Division 1 (8 inches)	16 inches
Division 2 (14 inches)	28 inches
Division 3 (20 inches)	40 inches

USDAA

Height	Length
12 inches	20 inches
16 inches	36 inches
22 inches	48 inches
26 inches	60 inches

In AKC, the broad jump is very similar to one found in obedience trials. It can be comprised of five 6-inch (15-cm) boards or four 8-inch (20-cm) boards that are 4 to 5 feet (1.2 m–1.5 m) long. It may be an ascending jump, which may rise in ½-inch (1.2 cm) increments, or it may be a hogback, where it rises to the center and then descends. Four posts mark the corners of the broad jump. The hogback is more diffi-

A Springer Spaniel clears the broad jump. Note: in most agility trials, the broad jump must have corner posts.

cult for smaller breeds that may not be able to see beyond the rise.

In UKC, the broad jump may be constructed from PVC or may be a UKC regulation broad jump. The UKC broad jump (also referred to as the long jump) can be comprised of two, three, or four 4 to 5-inch (10–13 cm) PVC pipes that are 3½ to 4 feet (1–1.5 m) long. Four posts mark the corners of the broad jump.

In USDAA, the broad jump is called the long jump. Four posts mark the corners of the jump.

The Platform Jump

The platform jump is an unusual jump that is special to UKC. It is constructed from two solid, low boxes with a short PVC jump between them. Ace must approach the

1. The platform jump. Lead Ace to the platform and have him sit on the platform box as this Shetland Sheepdog is doing.

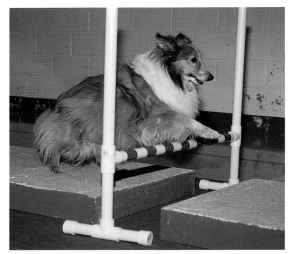

2. Command Ace to jump the small hurdle.

3. Give Ace the command to sit again.

platform. Simply lead him to the platform and have him sit on it and give him a treat. Give him the jump command and then put him in sit again and give him a treat. With practice, Ace will easily master the platform jump.

Wing Jumps and Other Jumps

Wing Jumps

jump and climb onto one of the platforms. He must then sit on his owner's command. Then he must jump the small hurdle and then sit on the opposite platform. This takes an extraordinary amount of control.

If Ace has never seen this type of jump before, he may become confused with the

All agility organizations have jumps with wings. Wings are side panels along each side of the jump that serve as decorations and handler restrictions. USDAA, AKC, and NADAC call out actual regulation sizes for wings, but UKC does not. They can be quite simple, such as a single panel, or very elaborate, such as a silhouette of a dog or cat, a trellis with flowers and vines, or a colorful banner.

Some dogs have difficulty with certain winged jumps. I've seen dogs that stopped in the middle of a trial run to investigate or bark at a dog silhouette. Some dogs may shy away from other winged jumps. If new things easily startle your dog, you may want to desensitize your dog to strange situations and obstacles.

Winged jumps may be difficult for the novice because they force the handler to work at a distance from her dog. It is not uncommon to see a novice dog try to jump the wings, instead of the actual hurdle. The only way to avoid this is to practice jumping with winged jumps.

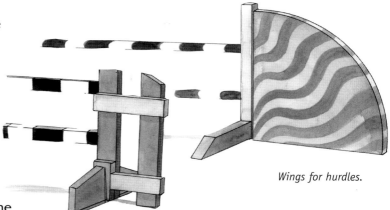

Wings for hurdles.

Wishing Well Jump

This jump is found only in USDAA courses. It is a jump in the shape of a wishing well (hence the name) that combines the tire and the spread hurdle. Teach the wishing well as you would the tire.

Bush Fence Hurdle

This jump is found in UKC courses. The hurdle consists of plants and lattice that reach 8-, 14-, and 20-inch (20, 35, 51 cm) jump heights.

Wishing well hurdle.

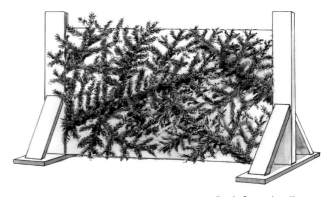

Bush fence hurdle.

The author's Alaskan Malamute, Kiana, demonstrates jumping over the log hurdle.

Log Hurdle

This jump is found in UKC courses. The log hurdle consists of 4-inch (10 cm) PVC pipes arranged in a pyramid structure. The pyramid may be arranged in 8-, 14-, or 20-inch (20, 35, 51 cm) heights.

Picket Fence Hurdle

This jump is found in UKC courses. The hurdle consists of interchangeable panels that resemble a picket fence. The sections are 8-, 14-, and 20-inch (20, 35, 51 cm) jump heights.

Rail Fence Hurdle

This jump is found in UKC courses. The hurdle consists of several PVC or narrow wooden cross rails. The rails are set to 8-, 14-, and 20-inch (20, 35, 51 cm) jump heights.

Water Hurdle

This jump is found in UKC courses. It is a long jump with a 6-inch (15 cm) high box filled with water in the middle. Two ramps, no more than 12 inches (30 cm) long are placed along each side to construct a 10-, 20-, or 30-inch (25, 51, 76 cm) long jump.

Chapter 10

The Tunnels

Teaching Tunnels

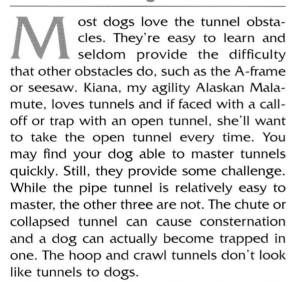

Most dogs love the tunnel obstacles. They're easy to learn and seldom provide the difficulty that other obstacles do, such as the A-frame or seesaw. Kiana, my agility Alaskan Malamute, loves tunnels and if faced with a call-off or trap with an open tunnel, she'll want to take the open tunnel every time. You may find your dog able to master tunnels quickly. Still, they provide some challenge. While the pipe tunnel is relatively easy to master, the other three are not. The chute or collapsed tunnel can cause consternation and a dog can actually become trapped in one. The hoop and crawl tunnels don't look like tunnels to dogs.

Choose a distinct word for each tunnel. It is not uncommon to have a pipe tunnel next to a closed tunnel in open and excellent trial courses. If you use the same word for different obstacles, you risk confusing Sierra and having her go off course.

If Sierra ever becomes trapped in a tunnel, get her out immediately. Trapped dogs will panic and often make their situation worse. When trying to extricate a trapped dog, keep away from the dog's teeth. Work on the chute fabric to provide an opening,

straighten the open tunnel, or pull the crawl tunnel off—whatever it takes. At a trial, you will get a nonqualifying score for touching the equipment and the dog, but that really won't matter. Take your dog, give her a hug, and lead her out of the ring. Don't try to force her back through the tunnel or do anything scary at least for a little while. If Sierra becomes trapped while training, spend some time playing with her first and then work on other obstacles for a while.

Dogs remember bad experiences. If Sierra becomes trapped in a tunnel, she may not wish to do the tunnel again for some time. In this case, start at the beginning and retrain your dog. With a little perseverance, your dog will be running through tunnels again.

Occasionally, you will find an open or closed tunnel disguised as a dog house. The disguise surprises some dogs and they may refuse to perform the obstacle because they do not recognize it. If new things scare Sierra, you may want to practice on a variety of equipment to get her used to accepting them.

Do not rush your dog through learning the obstacles. The obstacles seem easy to you because you understand how they work. Sierra, as smart as she may be, does not have that advantage. This is all very new and possibly scary.

Certain breeds do have a tendency toward being more successful in agility. The Golden Retriever is one such breed.

The Open or Pipe Tunnel

AKC

24 inches maximum diameter,
10 to 20 feet in length, 15 feet preferred

NADAC

24 inches diameter, 10 to 20 feet in length

UKC

approximately 24 inches diameter,
approximately 16 feet in length (Model 1)
OR approximately 16 by 28 inches wide,
square, and approximately 16 feet in
length (Model 2)

USDAA

24 inches diameter, 10 to 20 feet in length.
4 inch maximum spacing of wire ribs

When you start training tunnels, start with the open or pipe tunnel first. It is the easiest tunnel and will help build your dog's confidence. The open or pipe tunnel is a long tunnel with open ends on each side. Most pipe tunnels are made from tough fabric or plastic and have wire reinforcement. The only exception to this is Model 2 of the UKC open tunnels. It looks like two collapsed tunnels put together with a 30-degree bend.

When teaching a tunnel, shorten the tunnel as much as possible and make it straight through. Two people should be handling the dog at this time, one on each end of the tunnel. Your helper should be with Sierra to

The open or pipe tunnel.

That was easy. Reward Sierra for coming through.

hold her at the mouth of the tunnel. Do not have the helper try to force Sierra into the tunnel or crowd her. If Sierra thinks she is trapped, she may panic and bite. The helper's job is to only hold Sierra there while you coax Sierra through the tunnel from the other side. If Sierra shows any distress, have the helper let go and stand back.

Put a tracking lead on Sierra and thread the leash through the shortened tunnel. Don't toss food or treats into the tunnel try-ing to lure the dog in and don't crowd a dog. Now call Sierra and offer a bit of food. You may tug on the leash toward you if Sierra appears reluctant. Some people crawl part way into the tunnel to meet their dogs half way. Eventually, Sierra will decide it might be *OK* to crawl through. Use the word *tunnel* or some other word to signal that you want her to go into the tunnel.

Make a big fuss over Sierra and give her a treat when she has gotten through her

Shorten the tunnel as much as possible and make it straight through. Put a tracking leash on Sierra and thread the leash through. Coax Sierra through the tunnel as Raider the Alaskan Malamute and his owner demonstrate.

Lengthen the tunnel as your dog becomes more comfortable with it.

Finally, as Sierra builds confidence, add a curve.

The closed, collapsed, or chute tunnel.

first tunnel. Sierra will no doubt wonder what the fuss is about. Work with Sierra a few more times until she enters the tunnel without you having to tug her through. (Be sure to give her a treat after each successful completion.) Soon Sierra will enter the shortened tunnel without the leash. Start lengthening the tunnel, a little at a time until Sierra is completely comfortable with performing the tunnel in this configuration.

Next, add a slight bend to the tunnel. Sierra may be a little hesitant to enter where she cannot see the exit. If she is, decrease the bend further until it is almost straight through. Continue adding a little more bend to the tunnel when Sierra is comfortable with the current configuration. Eventually, you will have the tunnel bent into a semicircle where you will direct her to which entrance you wish her to enter.

The Closed, Collapsed, or Chute Tunnel

AKC

24 inches diameter or 24-inch by 24-inch opening; entrance section 24 to 36 inches long, ±2 inches; chute width goes from diameter opening to 96 inches at end flare; chute length 12 to 15 feet.

NADAC

minimum 22 inches diameter opening; entrance section maximum length 30 inches; chute width goes from diameter opening to 86 to 90 inches at end flare; chute length is maximum 8 feet long.

UKC

24 inches diameter (Model 1) or 28 by 14 inch opening (Model 2); entrance section 24 to 36 inches long (Model 1) or 24 inches (Model 2); chute minimum width 86 inches at flare (Model 1) or 72 inches wide (Model 2); chute length is approximately 10 feet (Model 1) or 13 to 14 feet (Model 2).

USDAA

18 to 24 inches diameter opening; entrance section 30 inches long; chute width Goes from diameter of opening to 65 to 96 inches at end flare; chute length is 12 feet.

The closed, collapsed, or chute tunnel is a little more challenging than the pipe tunnel. Once the dog learns the closed tunnel, it quickly becomes a favorite. Kiana loves the closed tunnel because she considers it some canine version of peek-a-boo. The closed tunnel is usually a barrel with a long piece of parachute fabric sewn into an 8- to 12-foot long chute or collapsed tunnel at the end. Dogs entering the chute enter through the barrel opening and then push their way through the parachute fabric to the end opening. This seems intimidating at first because the tunnel appears to have no

Avoid getting your dog tangled in the chute by keeping it flat.

1. Have your handler hold your dog at the entrance. Xena, the Bulldog, demonstrates.

exit. All organizations use the barrel and chute except the UKC, which has an alternative closed tunnel design with wickets and chute fabric.

Always be sure that the chute fabric on the closed tunnel is straight and laying flat before allowing your dog to enter. Many dogs will twist or bunch the fabric as they run through, making the chute hazardous for the next dog. If Sierra becomes caught in the fabric, she may panic and injure herself or the people trying to free her. Should Sierra ever get caught in the chute, get her out of there. Don't wait to see if she can free herself because she may make the situation worse.

2. Roll up most of the chute fabric to create a mini-pipe tunnel. Call Sierra through the tunnel.

3. Lengthen the chute after your dog becomes more comfortable with it. You will want to slowly drop the fabric so that the dog has to push through.

Start teaching the closed tunnel by rolling up most of the chute fabric and creating a mini pipe tunnel. Hold the chute end open while your helper holds Sierra at the barrel end. Thread Sierra's tracking leash through the opening. Call Sierra to you and use a unique word to describe the tunnel. Many people use *chute.* If Sierra has learned the pipe tunnel, she should come readily through the chute. If she does not, tug gently on the leash and call to her. Do not allow the handler to crowd or push Sierra into the tunnel. Some dogs may feel cornered with this. As Sierra comes through the other end, allow the fabric to drop on her shoulders so she gets a feeling for the fabric's weight. Praise and reward her each time she comes through the chute.

Once Sierra is comfortable going through the tunnel with it open, hold the chute so it sags a bit. Sierra will have to push on it more and nose her way through. If she shows any hesitation, open the tunnel a little more until she is comfortable with the new obstacle. After each successful run, lengthen the chute a little each time. Even-

4. As your dog approaches, allow the chute to drop on her back.

tually, you will be able to direct Sierra into a completely closed tunnel.

Even after Sierra has demonstrated that she can perform the closed tunnel, direct her into the opening and run beside her as she runs through the chute. Give her words of encouragement as she runs through. Some dogs become nervous when they can't see or hear you and may try to turn around in the chute. During training, I often touch Kiana's back while she is in the chute to let her know that I am beside her. While I cannot do this during a trial, Kiana is confident enough with my voice to perform the closed tunnel.

The Hoop Tunnel

UKC

Eight hoops. Approximately 30 to 32 inches high; 120 inches long; 30 inches wide. Hoops are set at 60-degree angles to one another.

The hoop tunnel, as its name implies, is a tunnel constructed from eight PVC hoops tied to a PVC frame. It is the least intimidating of the tunnels but can be difficult to master because it does not look like a tunnel to a dog. Often a dog will pop out of the side rather than go straight through.

Teach the hoop tunnel as you would a normal pipe tunnel. Start by putting a tracking lead on Sierra and threading the lead through the tunnel. Have a handler at one end hold Sierra while you go to the tunnel's far end. Tell Sierra "Sierra, hoop!" or whatever word you choose for the hoop tunnel and call her through. Use the leash as a guide to prevent Sierra from popping out of

1. Teach the hoop tunnel as you would a normal pipe tunnel. Thread the leash through. Bob, the Schipperke, and owner demonstrate.

2. Call your dog through, using food and praise. Don't allow her to pop out of the hoops.

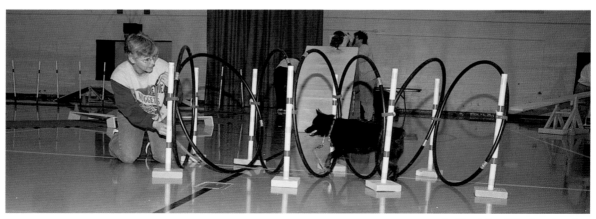

3. Give lots of food and praise.

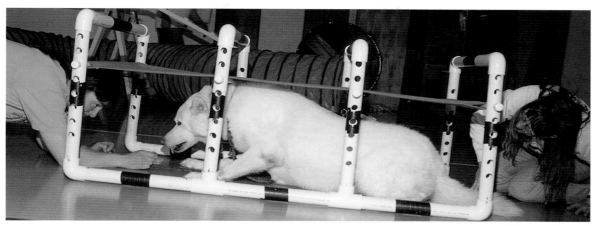

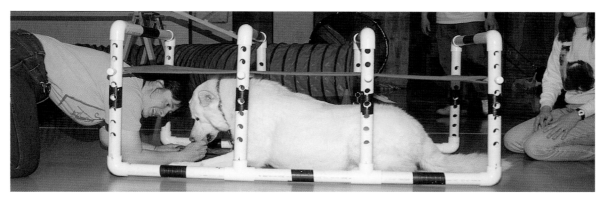

The crawl tunnel.

1. From a down stay *in front of the crawl tunnel, thread the leash through and lure your dog into the crawl tunnel. Kiana, the Alaskan Malamute, and the author demonstrate.*

the side. Praise and reward her for every successful completion.

One problem with hoop tunnels is their ability to shift. Usually a dog knocks a hoop or two out of place and it no longer looks like a tunnel. Always make certain the hoops are in their proper place or you will encourage her to exit at the sides.

Once you are working off-leash and Sierra decides to exit the hoop tunnel at the side, put Sierra back on a tracking leash and work with her on a proper exit. You should also work on your approaches toward obstacles. Many times the dog's exit is

dependent on her entrance. Always approach the hoop tunnel straight on, even if you have to take a moment to line your dog up.

The Crawl Tunnel

UKC

72 inches long; 8, 12, 16, 20, or 24 inches high depending on chest of dog; 30 inches wide.

Crawl Tunnel Divisions

	Crawl Tunnel Heights	Depth of Chest
Division 1	8 inches	up to and including 7 inches.
	12 inches	over 7 inches and up to and including 10 inches.
Division 2	12 inches	over 7 inches and up to and including 10 inches.
	16 inches	over 10 inches and up to and including 14 inches.
Division 3	16 inches	over 10 inches and up to and including 14 inches.
	20 inches	over 14 inches.

The crawl tunnel is possibly the most difficult tunnel to master. This tunnel doesn't look like a tunnel with its huge frame and fabric across it. The object of the crawl tunnel is for your dog to enter underneath and to crawl through and out.

Set the height to be one size higher than the normal height division before attempting to teach the crawl tunnel. Put a tracking lead on Sierra and thread the leash along the ground through the crawl tunnel. Put Sierra in a down-stay close to the entrance and have a handler hold her while you go to the far side. Call Sierra and give her light tugs to come to you. She may balk, seeing the crossbars before her. Have your handler

lure her lower by holding a treat at her nose and then luring her down and into the tunnel. Once the handler gets Sierra a little ways into the crawl tunnel, call Sierra and lure her out with a treat. Always praise and reward her when she performs the obstacle correctly.

You may have to work slowly with Sierra before she will attempt the crawl tunnel. Once she is comfortable with the current crawl tunnel height, lower the tunnel to the regulation height. If you have been working her at the greater height, she should have no difficulty adjusting to the lower height. If she does, train her as you did when you set the crawl tunnel to the greater height.

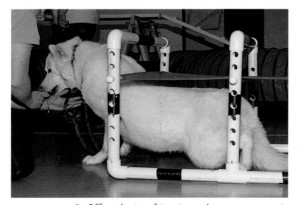
2. Offer plenty of treats and encouragement.

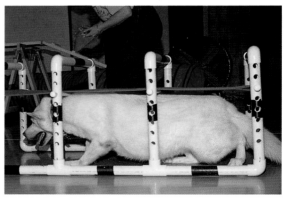
Kiana demonstrates the crawl tunnel.

Chapter 11
The Pause Table

Teaching Your Dog to Love the Table

The pause table and pause box are simple obstacles. The pause table is a table that adjusts to the various regulation heights. The dog must climb up on the table and perform a sit or down for the judge's count. The dog cannot stand up or move from the position or the count resumes. Unlike such obstacles like the teeter or weave poles, there isn't much of a technical challenge to the table, other than the sit-stay or down-stay. With some dogs, this alone might be the challenge, especially when there are many other much more fun obstacles!

The pause box is similar to the table, except it is a box constructed from PVC. Ace may not even recognize it as an obstacle and may walk across it. Like the table, Ace must perform a sit or down for the judge's count.

Teaching Ace the table is easy. Have the table set at a lower height than regulation. Put a leash on Ace's flat collar and lead him to the table. Say *Table!* or a word that depicts the table's uniqueness and lead him onto it. If Ace is not reliable on his sit or down-stays now is a good time to make him reliable—for at least 5 seconds. Give him the sit or down-stay (USDAA requires down-stay only). Count aloud: "Five-four-three-two-one-go!" Tell him "Good Dog!" and give him a treat. If Ace shows any hesitation over the table, you may have to give him the command, give him a treat once he hops on the table, and then give him a treat when he is finished performing the table.

Do not reward Ace for jumping off the table! You can use a release word such as "OK" or "all right," but do not give Ace much praise or a treat after he has jumped off. Otherwise, he may associate the act of jumping off the table with praise or a reward.

After Ace becomes comfortable with the table, switch to the regulation height and practice with that. If Ace requires a 24-inch table, be certain to practice with that regulation height. Many dogs that are comfortable with a 16-inch height table may initially refuse a 24-inch table.

Training for the pause box is very similar to training for the table. Use the same method to teach Ace to hop into the pause box, have him do a sit-stay or down-stay for the count, and then release.

You can train Ace to take the pause table or pause box from a distance. Have a trainer or handler—someone to whom Ace isn't necessarily attached—stand beside the table. Give the handler some treats. Tell Ace *Table!* or *Box!* depending on the obstacle. When Ace hops on the table or in the box, have the handler give Ace the treat. Practice this a few

A Golden Retriever demonstrates the pause table.

16 inches for 16- and 20-inch divisions; 24 inches for 24-inch division.

UKC

3–3½ feet square top; adjustable to UKC jump heights.

USDAA

36 inches square top; adjustable to 12, 16, and 24 inches.

The pause table is a table with a 3-foot square top (although in UKC, there can be a 3½ foot square top) and adjustable legs. The top is covered with a nonslip surface—either nonslip paint, industrial grade carpet, or rubber matting. (See each organization's rules regarding carpet on the table.) The dog must perform a sit or down on the table, depending on the organization's rules and the judge's choice.

times to have Ace looking to get up on the table to get a treat from the handler. Then take Ace a little farther away and tell him *Table!* (or *Box!*). You may have to take the first few steps before stopping and allowing Ace to continue toward the table. When Ace hops on the table or in the box, have the handler treat him and then put Ace in a sit or down position. Do this a few times to get Ace used to handling the table from a distance.

In UKC, the pause table and pause box have a special twist to them. They have color-coded sides. The dog must enter on one color and exit on another, depending on the judge's preference.

The Pause Table

AKC

36 inches square top. 8 inches high for 8-inch and 12-inch divisions;

The Pause Box

UKC

48 inches square; height 4–6 inches.

The pause box is only seen in UKC AGII and AGIII competition. It is a square box made from PVC or wood with 4–6 inch high sides. The pause box requires the handler to direct Ace to the correct side of the pause box and to enter from that side. The judge selects the sit or down beforehand. It is performed in the same way as a pause table, only on the ground. Many dogs may not see the pause box as an obstacle because of its lowness to the ground.

Chapter 12

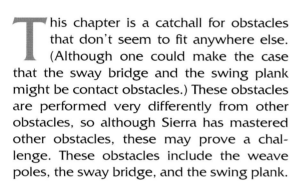

Miscellaneous Obstacles

This chapter is a catchall for obstacles that don't seem to fit anywhere else. (Although one could make the case that the sway bridge and the swing plank might be contact obstacles.) These obstacles are performed very differently from other obstacles, so although Sierra has mastered other obstacles, these may prove a challenge. These obstacles include the weave poles, the sway bridge, and the swing plank.

The Weave Poles

AKC

6 to 12 poles, 20–24 inches apart.
1 to 1¼ inch diameter. Minimum
36 inches high.

NADAC

20–21 inches apart. ¾–1 inch diameter.
36–48 inches in height.

UKC

9 poles, 24 or 25 inches apart. ½ inch
(⅞ inch) or 1 inch (1.5 inch) PVC. 3 or
4 feet in height.

USDAA

8 to 12 poles, 18–21 inches apart.
1 inch diameter. Minimum 3 feet high.

Most dogs have a difficult time learning the weave poles. The weave poles are usually not a physically challenging obstacle (except perhaps for the largest dogs), but they require the dog to learn to weave through them—something a dog would not normally do. There are 6 to 12 poles set 18 to 25 inches apart in a straight line. Sierra must enter them right to left (with the first pole on Sierra's left) and then weave through them.

There are several ways to teach the weave poles. The method explained here requires either stick-in-the-ground weave poles, a set of training weave poles (that can be set at different angles), or two sets of six freestanding weave poles. You must practice weave poles every day or every other day, unlike other obstacles, otherwise Sierra will not become proficient with them.

Set up the poles in a staggered column so that they are spaced wide enough for Sierra to walk through. They should be Sierra's shoulder width. Put a leash on Sierra's flat collar and lead her through the channel. Use the command *Weave!* or another command that you have chosen for the weave poles. Give her a treat and praise her when she successfully completes the channel. Work on this three or four times before dinner or breakfast—you need not have several repetitions at a session.

A Border Collie demonstrates the weave poles.

Once Sierra has become comfortable with the columns, remove the leash and send her through. Give her the command *Weave!* beforehand and give her a treat after she runs through the channel. Work with Sierra in this configuration for a week to two weeks until she is confident. Now, move the poles in one inch on each side.

If you have properly spaced the poles to Sierra's shoulder width, this next exercise will force her to bend a little. Give Sierra the weave command and give her a treat. If she was confident with the channel, she should have no problem with the narrower channel. If she does, go back to the last step and repeat it for a week. Practice the weave poles in this configuration for a week to two weeks until Sierra becomes completely comfortable with performing the weave poles in the current configuration. Then move the poles in another inch.

Start teaching weave poles by aligning the poles in a column and running Ace through it. After two weeks, as Ace becomes proficient, move the poles one inch inward. This will cause Ace to bend to get through the column. Every two weeks, until the poles are in the final configuration, move the poles in one inch and practice with that every day.

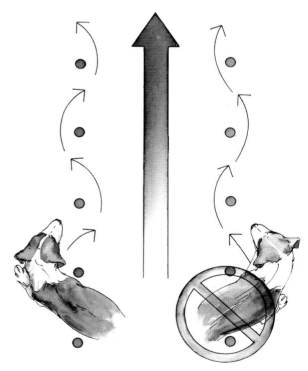

The right and wrong way to enter weave poles. Always enter right to left so that the farthest pole is on Ace's right.

1. Start your training weave poles at least shoulder width or farther. Lead Sierra through the poles as the author and Kiana, the Alaskan Malamute, demonstrate. Train for a few minutes every day on the weave poles.

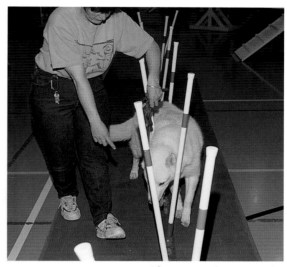

3. After two weeks, narrow the poles again and train on that.

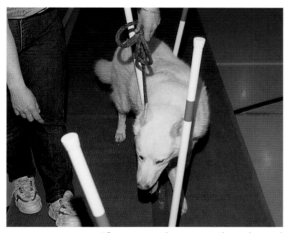

2. After two weeks, narrow the poles and train on the new configuration. Sierra will have to bend to get through.

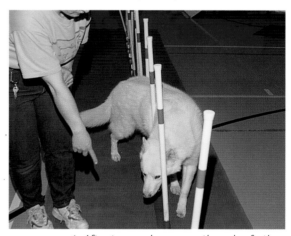

4. After two weeks, narrow the poles further. Note how Kiana must bend to perform these poles. Practice this configuration for two weeks.

The trick to this method is repetition and moving the weave poles gradually to their correct configuration. This method requires patience on the part of the handler. It is tempting to have Sierra run through the channels once or twice, declare her ready to move onto the next step and then the next step and then discover Sierra really doesn't weave well. It takes weeks, if not months, to teach a dog to weave properly. If Sierra catches on, you might be able to forego the months, but it will still take weeks. Be patient!

This is certainly not the only way to teach weave poles. Some methods, such as those

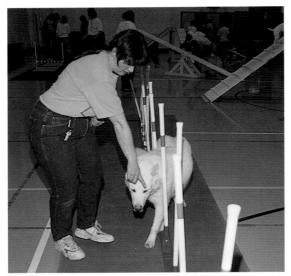

5. Almost in final configuration. Practice this configuration for two weeks as well.

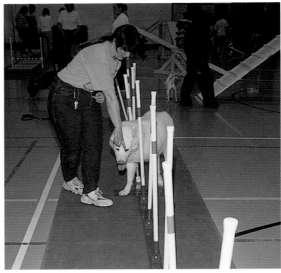

6. Weaving in the final configuration.

using clicker training, break down the weaving action into small components and reward the dog for each completed maneuver.

The Sway Bridge

UKC

Bridge surface—19 inches wide, 6.5 or 8 feet long, constructed of 2 by 2 boards. Ramps are 24 by 48 inches.

The sway bridge is a UKC obstacle that resembles a suspended bridge with multiple planks between two short ramps. When a dog crosses the sway bridge, the dog's weight causes the planks to sway from side to side and shift up and down. Dogs dislike movement and are more likely to hop off than complete the obstacle.

The trick to teaching the sway bridge is to minimize the movement. You will need one or two extra handlers to help keep the sway bridge steady. Have one person stand on

The sway bridge.

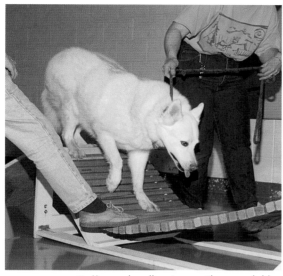

1. Have a handler step on the sway bridge while you lead Sierra across. The author's Malamute, Kiana, demonstrates.

2. Lead your dog over the sway bridge confidently.

the opposite side of the sway bridge, halfway through the obstacle. They will need to step on the bridge's planks with one foot, allowing their weight to steady

the bridge. If you have a second person to help, have them ready along the opposite side to be sure that Sierra will not jump off as she walks across it.

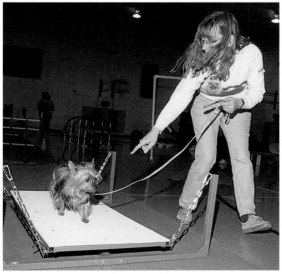

1. Lead Sierra quickly over the swing plank. Gwendolyn, the Yorkshire Terrier, demonstrates.

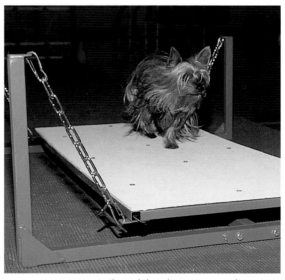

2. Gwendolyn demonstrates the proper way of performing the swing plank.

A German Shepherd Dog on the swing plank.

Attach a short leash or tab to Sierra's flat collar and lead her with a straight approach towards the sway bridge. Say *Bridge!* or *Sway!* or a command that is unique to the sway bridge and then lead her over. Lead her over the bridge quickly while having your handler spot her on the other side. Give Sierra plenty of praise and a treat if she finishes the obstacle.

Don't allow your dog to stop on the swing plank as it may panic him.

Some dogs may panic on the sway bridge. Don't force Sierra through it if she starts to panic. Use treats as lures and move swiftly over the bridge. Don't stop—this allows your dog to freeze and causes the sway bridge to swing more violently. It helps for a dog to be accustomed to a moving object beforehand, such as the swing plank or the teeter-totter.

The Swing Plank

UKC

Plank surface—4 feet long and approximately 20 inches wide.
Uprights are 15 inches.

The swing plank is another UKC obstacle. This obstacle consists of a large non-skid surfaced plank that is attached to four uprights using a chain or cable. When the dog steps on the swing plank, the plank swings with the weight. In order for Sierra to perform this obstacle correctly, she must travel across it and put all four feet on the plank.

Start teaching the swing plank by snapping a leash on Sierra's flat collar and leading her quickly over the plank. Choose a command such as *Plank!* or *Swing!* as the command. Use plenty of praise and encouragement. Don't stop or go slowly over the plank—like the sway bridge, this can cause Sierra to panic if she is able to stop and think about her predicament. Give her treats and praise when she completes it.

Like the sway bridge, the swing plank is best left for more accomplished and confident dogs. Sierra should be familiar with the teeter-totter before learning the swing plank.

Chapter 13

Putting Together a Simple Home Agility Course

You don't need a lot of money to put together some items that will serve as a home agility course. You can construct simple bar hurdles, weave poles, and the tire obstacle from PVC pipes. You can purchase appropriate substitutes for complex items, such as the table and tunnel and achieve a good simulation. Use your imagination. This is strictly for fun and practice. If you wish to construct your own regulation-style equipment, there are many good books with plans available, including *Hoga Agility, Do-It-Yourself Plans for Constructing Dog Agility Articles* by Jim Hutchens (self-published).

Tools Needed

You'll need the following tools to construct equipment:
- hacksaw
- PVC pipe cutter, capable of cutting pipe up to 2 inches
- drill
- clamps
- workbench
- taps
- vice clamp

Bar Jumps

The bar jumps are perhaps the simplest to construct of all home agility equipment. For constructing a bar jump, you will need the following:

2—10-foot lengths of 1-inch schedule 40 PVC cut as follows:

    2 pieces 36 inches long
    1 piece 49 inches long
    1 piece 48 inches long
    4 pieces 12 inches long
    2 pieces 8 inches long
    2 pieces 3 inches long

2—1-inch PVC tees
4—1-inch PVC ells
6—1-inch PVC caps
Colored electrical tape
PVC cement

TIP: Safety First!

Take precautions whenever you use hand tools. Be certain to wear eye protection while cutting and drilling and always use clamps to hold the project you're working on.

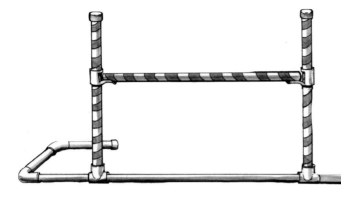

Finished bar jump.

8. With a permanent marker, mark a two-inch long by one-inch wide square that extends from the base of the 3-inch PVC pipe.

9. With a hacksaw, carefully cut through one side of the PVC pipe along one side of the mark. (Note: You will need clamps and a workbench for this.)

10. Cut along the top of the square and then carefully cut until you are about ½ inch away from cutting through. Carefully bend the square out.

11. Do the same to the other 3-inch PVC pipe.

12. With a measuring tape, mark the following jump heights on the 36-inch uprights: 8-inch, 12-inch, 16-inch, 20-inch, 24-inch, and 26-inch.

13. Slide the 3-inch cut PVC over the uprights to the marks. The fit will be snug. Have the bent squares facing the same direction. This will hold the crossbar.

14. Fit the 48-inch crossbar with end caps.

15. Wrap colored electrical tape to provide visibility on uprights and crossbar.

16. Once the jump is completed, use PVC cement to secure all parts or leave as is to provide easy transport.

1. Cut the PVC using PVC cutters or hacksaw with vice clamps.

2. Assemble the base legs as follows:
   a) Use two 12-inch PVC pipes and connect them together with an ell.
   b) Use one of the 8-inch PVC pipes and connect it to another ell and to one of the 12-inch PVC that you assembled in the step a) to form a "C."
   c) Repeat steps a) and b) so that you have two "C" assemblies.
   d) Fit end caps into the 8-inch PVC ends.

3. Invert both tees and connect one side of the inverted "T" to the 49-inch bar.

4. Connect one of the "C" base legs at the 12-inch PVC pipe to the other side of the "T."

5. Connect the other "C" base legs in the same fashion on the other side, but make it curve to the other side of the base. The base should look somewhat "S" shaped. (See Diagram.)

6. Insert the two 36-inch PVC pipes into the tee's fitting.

7. Fit end caps into the tops of the 36-inch PVC.

Tunnel

Tunnels are not easy to make. However, you can purchase a cheap tunnel from various children's toy stores. These are very inexpensive and you can purchase several.

You can find inexpensive tunnels at children's toy stores or purchase one directly from an agility supplier.

Tire

3—10-foot lengths of 1½-inch schedule 40
PVC cut as follows:
> 2 pieces 48 inches long
> 2 pieces 60 inches long
> 2 pieces 4 inches long
> 4 pieces 12 inches long

2—1½ inch ells
4—1½ inch tees
4—1½ inch end caps
1—piece of 4-inch drainage pipe cut to
98 inches long
1—internal connector for drainage pipe
Duct tape, any color
Electrical tape, contrasting colors
3—Adjustable bungee cords
PVC cement

1. Cut the PVC using a PVC pipe cutter or
hacksaw, using vice clamps.

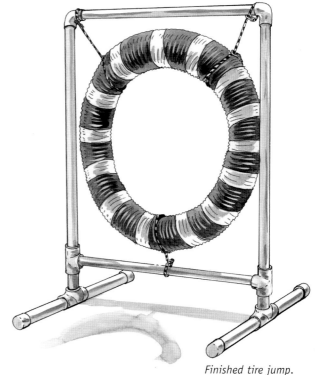

Finished tire jump.

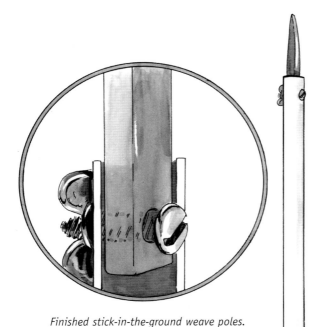

Finished stick-in-the-ground weave poles.

2. To make the legs, fit the 12-inch PVC into the inverted "T" of the tees. Cap them with end caps.

3. Fit the 4-inch PVC pipes into the top portion of the inverted tees.

4. Turn the other two tees sideways and fit one into the top of each 4-inch PVC pipe. Be certain the bases of the tees are facing each other.

5. Fit a 48-inch crossbar into the two tees.

6. Fit the two 60-inch uprights into the two tees' ends.

7. Fit each end of the 60-inch upright with an ell.

8. Fit a 48-inch crossbar into the ell.

9. Once assembled, use PVC cement to make the joints permanent.

10. For the tire:

   a) Fit ends of drainage pipe together using internal connector

   b) Wrap with duct tape.

   c) Try wrapping one section with electrical tape of a contrasting color (yellow) and then another section with a different color (red or orange)

11. Mount tire using adjustable bungees, two on the top corners and one on the bottom.

12. To measure the jump height, measure from the bottom of the tire's inside to the floor.

Weave Poles

It is quite easy to construct stick-in-the-ground weave poles by purchasing fiberglass tent stakes (available at camping or sporting goods stores) and cutting 12 pieces of 36-inch long, ¾-inch schedule 40 PVC and slipping them over the tent stakes. You can make this more permanent by cutting the tent poles to 8 inches long (retaining the pointed end) and drilling two holes through both the tent poles and the PVC pipe. Use bolts with washers and locking nuts to bolt the fiberglass tent poles to the PVC.

Table

Instead of trying to build a table, you can use many objects as a substitute. A wooden pallet with a plywood top will work well for dogs jumping 8-inch heights. Adjustable grooming tables, available from pet supply stores, will function as a table suitable for training on. Make certain that whatever you use is steady and can support the weight of your dog.

PART THREE

PUTTING IT ALL TOGETHER

Chapter 14

Handling and Sequencing

Once Ace is confident with the obstacles, he is ready to learn coursework. Many beginning handlers, once their dogs become somewhat proficient with the obstacles, are convinced that their dog is ready for competition. Nothing could be further from the truth! Agility is not just running over obstacles. Agility is teamwork. You and your dog should be able to do the following consistently before you enter an agility trial:

- You must be able to direct your dog to an obstacle, both close up and from a distance, with verbal and nonverbal signals.
- You must be able to handle your dog from the left or right sides, depending on the course.
- You must be able to call the dog towards and direct the dog away from you.
- You should be able to perform crossovers and cross-behinds smoothly, without disrupting your dog's rhythm.
- You must be able to work in varying environments with various distractions and still have control over your dog, even when he's off leash.

If you think that is quite a bit, you're right. Most beginning dogs seldom can do one or two reliably, let alone with great proficiency.

A clean run is 90 percent the dog and 10 percent the handler. A bad run is almost always the handler's fault. Either the handler

hasn't trained the dog properly, signaled the dog off course, gave incorrect signals, or has confused the dog. Remember that when *your* dog makes a mistake on the course, it is your fault, not his. You may be asking for something he hasn't learned, understood completely, or is incapable of doing (at this specific time or at any time, depending on the circumstance). For example, if your dog has been jumping well all day and then knocks over the bar or refuses the jump, he may be tired, sore, injured, or maybe has a thorn in his paw. It may be hot and he may need a drink of water or he may be feeling sick. It is up to you, the handler, to know your dog well enough to understand that he may not be feeling well.

When you begin working Ace, realize that you must first establish your own rhythm between your canine partner and yourself. This comes with time and practice. However, starting with good handling practices is one way to avoid bad techniques, unclear handling, and refusals.

The exercises presented in this chapter are intended to teach concepts. Ace may not get them right after the first time or even after several times. These exercises use *sequencing*—being able to deconstruct a course into manageable components. Technically, sequencing is putting together two or more obstacles, but trainers frequently use sequencing to learn how to

Exercise: Focusing on Your Hands

To get your dog to focus on your hands, try playing this little game. Hold a piece of bait in each hand, cupping the food with your thumb, but leaving your forefingers extended. Move your right hand in an arc parallel to the ground, either away from your body or towards your body. (You may have to first wave the bait in front of Ace's nose to entice him to follow it.) As Ace's nose follows it, give him a piece as a reward and shift hands to lure him in the opposite direction. When you run out of bait, skillfully slip another piece into the empty hand while you keep him preoccupied with the other one.

Ace will delight in this new game. It will make him focus on where you are directing him with your hands. Hand direction works well in noisy situations where you cannot always be heard. It also works well when the handler gets excited and stumbles over commands in excitement. I've called tunnels "teeter" and A-frames "walk it" more often than I care to admit. The hand signal verifies what you want your dog to do, although all you've been able to blurt out is "that blue thing."

handle parts of a course. Run-throughs are full courses. Most handlers learn to break complex courses into mini-courses or sequences to simplify a complex course.

You can practice most of these exercises at home with equipment from Chapter 11; however, if you have a full set of agility equipment, you can readily substitute another obstacle for a jump (unless its obvi-

ous the focus is on jumping techniques). Experiment and have fun.

Directing Your Dog Over Obstacles

Direct your dog to an obstacle by keeping your hand closest to the dog open and flat. Push your hand out towards the obstacle as though pushing it away. Say the name of the obstacle as you push towards it. At first, Ace may seem a little puzzled by this, but he will soon pick up your signals and come to expect them.

If you've ever trained for obedience, by now you are saying, "But don't you have to use a hand signal or a verbal command, not both?" No. That is the beauty of agility—you can use hand signals, wave your arms wildly, say the command over and over, and pray for a five second sit. However, there is a disqualification for overhandling and blocking in certain forms of agility, such as UKC and AKC. See Blocking and Overhandling in this chapter, Chapter 16 on Competition, and Chapter 17 on National Agility Trial Rules.

Timing of the command is critical. Most dogs are so fast that by the time you've said the obstacle's name, it's too late for the dog to commit. If Ace is a fast or average speed dog, you should be saying the next obstacle's name while the dog is completing the previous obstacle. For example, you should be saying "teeter" while Ace is mid-air on the broad jump (assuming the course goes broad jump to teeter).

This is, of course, ideal. You should also being giving the command once. In reality, every dog is different and may require different handling. Kiana, for example, will not remember the command for the next obstacle I've given at the previous obstacle and will perform a magnificent run-out. I have to match my handling to her speed and comprehension, using my hand to motion her toward a particular obstacle and then using the verbal command once she is lined up.

If you haven't stopped using Ace's name along with the command, do so. Ace is focused on you and the obstacles. Also, shorten each command, if feasible. *Ace, A-frame!* should become *frame*. *Ace, tire, over!* should become *tire*. And so on. In competition, you may not have the time to shout full sentences. Practice one word commands now.

Handling from the Right or Left Side

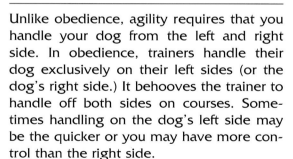

Unlike obedience, agility requires that you handle your dog from the left and right side. In obedience, trainers handle their dog exclusively on their left sides (or the dog's right side.) It behooves the trainer to handle off both sides on courses. Sometimes handling on the dog's left side may be the quicker or you may have more control than the right side.

If you and Ace trained in obedience, having Ace on your right side (the dog's left side) may feel strange and unnatural. You should practice training Ace on obstacles on both sides. Some judges intentionally build courses that naturally flow on the left side to present a challenge to right-sided only dogs.

Which side should you handle on? It depends, but generally, the correct answer is the side that allows you to travel minimally on the inside line of the course or obstacle. The inside line is not apparent with one obstacle, unless that obstacle is the tunnel. Usually it requires two or three obstacles set up in a sequence to determine which would be the most expedient path. Dogs are much faster than humans, so you will be the slowest member of the team. (If you aren't convinced your dog is faster than you, just try to chase him down sometime when he doesn't want to be caught.) In order to keep from holding up the team, you must figure out the most expedient path through the course.

The most expedient path may require handling on the right or left side. It may require handling on both sides. It may require crossovers and cross-behinds. By breaking a run-through into smaller components, you can analyze what might be the better way to take a particular run.

Do you always handle on the inside line of the course? Not necessarily. A number of factors such as course layout and the dog's training and ability may preempt handling on the inside line. For example, if the course leads you into a trap along the inside

TIP: Always Choose a Lower Jump Height in Sequencing Practice

When practicing sequencing, choose a lower jump height to avoid injury. Multiple jumps cause stress on the carpals and forelegs; higher jumps add additional stress plus may cause injury. Save full height for practice run-throughs.

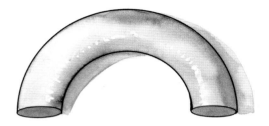

Practice obstacles for the next four exercises.

and right sides. The last exercise demonstrates how slow and cumbersome it can be when you choose to handle from the incorrect side. In this exercise, you will need a bar jump, a tunnel, and a tire jump or three bar jumps. In either configuration, you will be setting up the obstacles in an upside-down U pattern. The lower right part of the U is the first bar jump; the lower left part of the U is the tire jump. The tunnel will make up the curve of the U with its openings facing the two jumps. The dog should be able to jump the bar jump, enter the tunnel and then jump through the tire (or vice versa, depending on whether you run from right-

line that you know Ace will take, a better solution might be to choose the outside line and take a time fault instead of receiving an off course that could cost you points or disqualify you, depending on the style and class you run.

Handling Exercises— Handling from Both Sides

The following are three exercises designed to demonstrate how to handle from the left

Exercise: Handling from the Dog's Left Side

Start in front of the bar jump with Ace on your right side (you are on Ace's left side). You should have enough room so Ace can jump the bar hurdle. Ace will be jumping the bar hurdle, going through the tunnel, and then jumping through the tire. Give Ace the command to jump the hurdle. You will run along beside him on Ace's left side until just after the bar jump or right before the tunnel. Direct Ace to the tunnel and as soon as he completes the tunnel, direct him to the tire.

If the tunnel is too much of a trap, you can substitute the three hurdle combination instead. If you've chosen to use this set up, you should stop just after the first jump and direct Ace to each hurdle.

If you do this properly, even with a beginning dog, you should be taking less steps than if you had taken the outside line. (Try Exercise: Handling on the Outside Line to see the difference.)

TIP: Spend No More than 10 Minutes per Training Session

When you start focusing on exercises at home, spend no more than 10 minutes training and no more than three sessions a day. Longer training sessions tempt you to try to grind the lesson in instead of having fun. If you find yourself too focused on the training and Ace is not responding correctly, take a break and play with him. Then have him perform something he is good at, reward him with treats, and quit for the day.

to-left or left-to-right). The alternate configuration is two bar jumps at the lower right and left parts of the upside-down U with a bar jump perpendicular to the other two at the curve of the U.

Exercise: The *Here* Command

Once Ace knows *Here!* you can start putting it together with obstacles. Try the following: Take two bar jumps and put one in front of Ace and then set up another one so that Ace will have to turn 90 degrees left to take the other one. Put Ace in a sit before the first jump (leaving room so that he can jump it). Stand so you will be handling from Ace's left side.

Direct Ace over, *Ace, over!* When Ace is in mid-air, move forward and give Ace the *Come!* or *Here!* command. Ace should turn toward you and be lined up for the next jump. Direct Ace over the second jump.

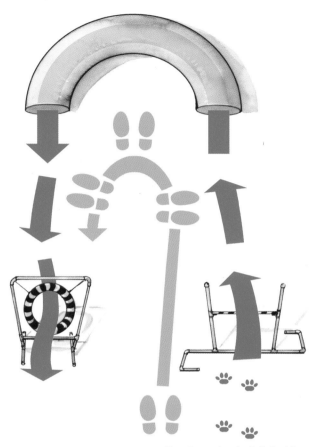

Handling from the dog's left side.

Here or *Come* Command

Your dog needs to know *Here* or *Come*. This is an easy command to teach. Every time you say *Here!*, offer a treat. Soon, you'll be able to call Ace from anywhere.

Kiana and I often play a game while we are waiting for our turn at a trial. I let her go out ahead of me and then call her back with a *Here!* command. I do this off leash in a

Handling from the dog's left side.

1. Start your dog on the bar hurdle and start turning toward the tunnel. Beau, the Bouvier De Flanders, and owner demonstrate.

2. As Ace exits the tunnel, turn to direct him toward the tire.

3. Send Ace through the tire.

Handling from the dog's right side.

1. Start your dog on the tire jump and start turning toward the tunnel. Paisley, the Australian Shepherd, and her handler demonstrate.

2. Send your dog to the tunnel.

3. Continue your turn and direct Ace toward the bar jump.

Exercise: Handling from the Dog's Right Side

This time, stand before the tire. You should be on Ace's right side now, facing the inside of the line. (Note: Obedience people may feel more comfortable with this arrangement.) Guide Ace through the tire, stopping yourself just beyond the tire and directing him into the tunnel. Then turn and give him the command over the bar jump.

Again, if the tunnel is too much of a trap, you can substitute the three hurdle combination instead. Regardless of which combination of obstacles you use, you should be able to move quickly enough to direct Ace to the obstacles without too many steps.

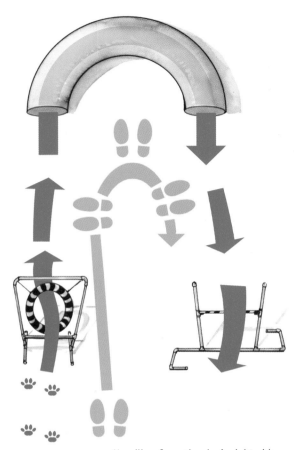

Handling from the dog's right side.

Teach your dog early on to watch your hands. Maya, the Bouvier De Flanders, and her owner demonstrate.

fenced in area. (Never turn your dog off leash in an open area—there is too great a risk for your dog to escape.) Practicing *Here!* at home is fun too. I may not have the prettiest sits in the world, but Kiana always comes running the moment I say *Here!*

Get Out Command

The *Get Out* command is the opposite of the *Here* command. You are asking your dog to go away from you rather than come towards you. Train Ace to *Get Out* with a ball, toy, or other prize, or use treats. Toss the toy or treat away from you and as he starts to chase it, say *Get Out!* (If Ace is the retrieving type, you can add a *Here!* and work on both commands simultaneously.)

Getting Your Dog to Lead Out

Teaching your dog to lead out is important, especially if you are not fast or the course requires you to head to another portion of the course while sending your dog ahead. You may wish to send Ace through the last

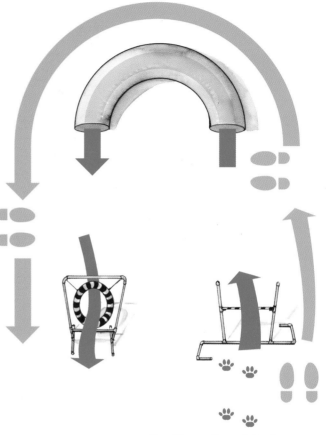

Handling on the outside line.

Exercise: Handling on the Outside Line

The previous two exercises focused on moving along the inside line. Now, you and Ace will stand in front of the bar jump, except you are now on Ace's right-hand side. Have Ace jump the bar and move forward along the right-hand side. Resist the urge to crossover at the tunnel and instead go around the tunnel on the right-hand side, directing Ace through the tunnel. Then direct Ace through the tire.

If Ace is a moderately fast (or faster) dog, you may have found yourself having trouble keeping up, especially at the tunnel. Ace may have arrived at the tire and may have run-out before you could direct him to it. This is why it is very important to choose your strategy carefully when on a run-through. In sequencing, handlers have the luxury of trying out new combinations before the trial.

two or three jumps and cross the finish line, not having him wait on you.

Place two jumps in sequence. Start by commanding him over the first jump. Once Ace is over the jump, stop a little before where you would normally stop and command Ace over the second jump. Be sure to use a pushing motion as your signal. Give Ace a treat and then try the jump sequence again, stopping a little earlier. Eventually, you should be able to stop at or before the first jump and command Ace over the second jump. This takes time and

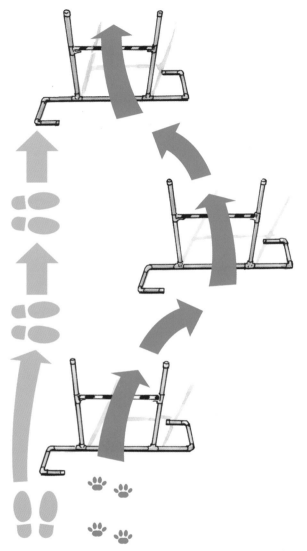

The get out *command.*

Exercise: The *Get Out* Command

Once Ace knows *Get out!* you can put it together with obstacles much the same way you did with *Here!* Set up three jumps in a row, only stagger the second to the right so that Ace must make an effort to divert his course to take it. Handle Ace from his left side.

Direct Ace over, *Ace, over!* When Ace is in mid air, move forward and give Ace the *Get Out* command. Ace should turn away from you and be lined up for the next jump. Direct Ace over the second jump. Now you can call him back with a *Here!* command and direct him over the jump with a third *Over!*

Tracy directs Karoo over a bar jump in a sequence.

patience. Ace may need many sessions before you can make even a little progress.

Once Ace feels comfortable with your handling from a shorter distance, you can slowly extend that distance. Anytime that Ace does not perform the obstacles cor-

Handling on the outside line.

1. Start by directing your dog through the tunnel. Becket, the Bearded Collie, and owner demonstrate.

2. While Ace enters the tunnel, run around the tunnel on the outside.

3. Becket is definitely faster than his owner. Ace will outrun you as well, unless he is small or slow.

4. Direct Ace over the bar hurdle.

The *Here* command.

1. Direct Ace over the first jump. You should be on Ace's left side. Lilac and her owner demonstrate.

2. Call "Here!" and direct Ace towards the second jump.

The *Get Out* command.

Use the get out *command to push your dog toward the second jump. Impi, the Norwegian Elkhound, and owner demonstrate.*

Leading out.
Start by commanding your dog over the first jump. Once Ace is over the jump, stop a little before where you would normally and command Ace over the second jump. Luna, the Italian Greyhound, demonstrates.

enough distance between Ace and the jump so he can clear it. Go around the jump and stand behind and to the side of it. Call Ace with either a *Here!* or *Come!* command. As he starts forward, tell him, *Ace, over!* Praise and reward him.

rectly, go back to the point he was comfortable with, and work with him at that level. Eventually, you should be able to extend the distance two or three jumps.

Recalling Your Dog Over Obstacles

Being able to recall your dog over obstacles is useful at the beginning of a course or run-through when there are a series of fast obstacles (jumps) followed by a slow obstacle (contact obstacle, weave poles). This is especially useful if Ace is a very fast dog or if you have difficulty keeping up with him because of an impaired ability to run.

Start training Ace with one bar jump. Put Ace in a sit-stay before the bar jump with

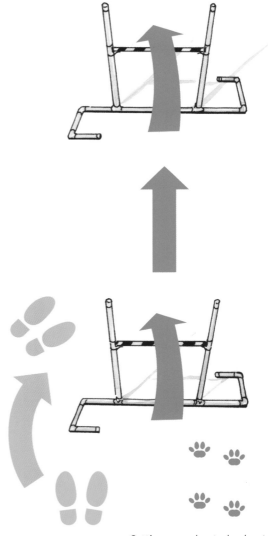

Getting your dog to lead out.

Recalling over obstacles.
*Call Ace with either a "Here!" or "Come!" command. Give Ace the "Over!" command
as he approaches the jump. Luna, the Italian Greyhound, and her owner demonstrate.*

If Ace becomes confused and goes around, try snapping a long line or flexi-lead to Ace's flat collar and stand in front of the bar jump holding the leash and allowing it to gently drape across the bar. Call Ace again and retract or reel in the line. As Ace approaches the jump, command him *Over!* If he balks because the bar is too high, set it lower and try again. Once Ace goes over the bar jump, praise and treat him.

Recalling over jumps.
1. Move out to the second jump and recall Ace over the jumps. Jeffrey and his owner demonstrate.

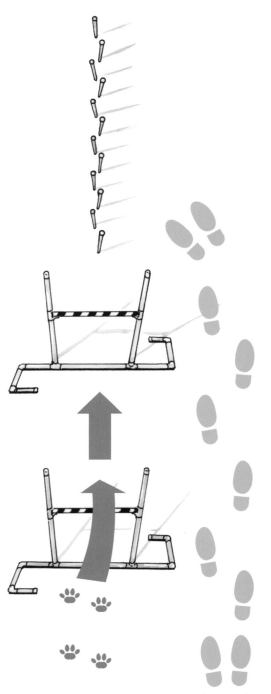

Recalling your dog over jumps.

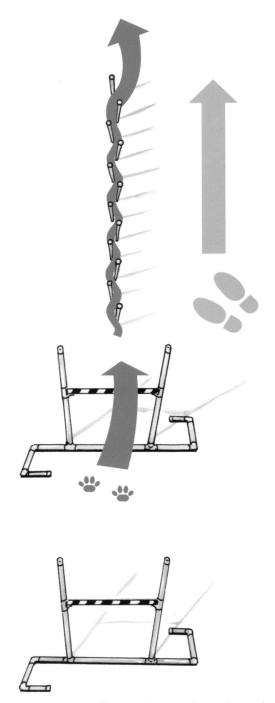

Recalling your dog over jumps (weaves).

2. Start moving the moment Ace clears the second jump.

Exercise: Recalling Your Dog Over Jumps

Set up either two jumps and weave pole or two jumps and a contact obstacle in sequence. Add a tunnel or another jump after the weave poles or contact obstacle. Put Ace in a sit-stay and walk out to the beginning of the weave poles or contact obstacle. (You can handle from either side.) Order Ace over the jumps and start moving with him with the weaves or contact obstacle and then over the jump or through the tunnel. Now try the same sequence while running next to Ace.

3. Move with Ace as he enters the weave poles.

Once Ace learns that you want him to go over the bar jump when you call him, recalling him over two or more should not be difficult. Ace must first become proficient with each jump before you add an additional one.

If Ace is an extremely fast dog, you will see how much easier it is to keep up with him by recalling him through the first two jumps, as opposed to running with him.

Crossovers and Cross-behinds

Crossovers and cross-behinds are necessary for handling. A crossover or cross-in-front is where the handler crosses in front of the dog before the dog reaches a piece of equipment. A cross-behind is where the handler crosses behind the dog, who is usually committed to a particular obstacle. Handlers use these techniques when the course changes its inside line. Get Ace used to cross-in-fronts and cross-behinds early so this handling technique does not surprise him when you do it on a course.

One of the best places to cross is at the pause table. Ace is at the table for 5 seconds, enabling you to change position while Ace is on the table or shortly thereafter. Good cross-behind obstacles include the tunnel and any contact obstacle (although you may cross-behind any obstacle, these give you a little time to get in position). You can cross in front of any obstacle, but be careful! You may find yourself nearly colliding into Ace, especially if Ace is fast.

Exercise: Cross-behind

Set up the following course in sequence as shown below: two bar jumps, tunnel in an L-shape configuration, bar jump, and then a bar jump set right 90 degrees. You should be handling from your right side or Ace's left side. Send Ace over the two jumps and through the tunnel. Cross by cutting past the tunnel's second opening so that you are now handling from your left side. (See page 116.) Now send Ace over the jump, turn 90 degrees right with the *Here* command, and send him over the last jump.

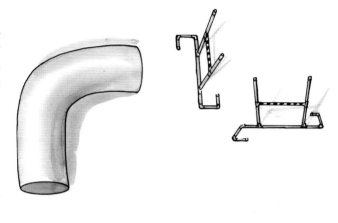

Crossovers and cross-behinds.

1. Cross-behind Ace as he enters the tunnel. Karoo, the Australian Cattle Dog, and her owner demonstrate.

2. Once you perform the cross-behind, direct Ace to the jump.

3. Call "Here!" on finishing the jump after the tunnel and direct Ace to the next jump at a 90 degree angle.

Exercise: Crossovers or Cross-in-front

Use the same set up as in the previous exercise. This time, run the sequence from the opposite direction. Begin handling with Ace on your right-hand side. Put Ace in a sit-stay and walk to the inside line between the first jump and the 90-degree left jump. Recall Ace over the first jump, call him with a *Here!* command and while moving past the second jump, command Ace over that. While Ace is in mid-air, cross in front of him and send him through the tunnel. Continue handling Ace on your left side through the other two jumps.

Right, Over! Left, Over! Teaching Ace to Know Right from Left

Teaching Ace to know right from left sounds like a parlor trick, but is a helpful way to have control over your dog. Start first by setting up two bar jumps side-by-side. Use the handling exercise on page 114 to warm up. Stand between the two jumps. Have Ace focus on your hands and command him over the right-side jump using the command *Right, Over!* or *Right, Jump!* Do the same with the left jump with *Left, Over!* or *Left, Jump!*

Cross in front of Ace before sending him through the tunnel. Aspen, a West Highland Terrier, and owner demonstrate.

Alternate between jumps and then mix them up. You should still be using definite hand signals. Once Ace is comfortable with the new exercise (this should take several days of 5 to 10 minutes of practice), start using less of the visual cue. If Ace hesitates at any time and looks confused, use more of the visual cue until he is comfortable enough to move on. With practice, you should be able to call Ace to the right or left.

where you wish your dog to go. Practice the exercise on page 114, if necessary, to teach Ace to focus on your hands. In many cases, the call-off may be one jump, where the next obstacle you must take is another jump.

If Ace has learned right from left, the call-off may be less troublesome. You may be able to direct him by saying "Ace, left over!" If Ace knows to turn left and look, he is likely to complete the jump rather than take the call-off.

Call-offs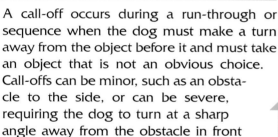

A call-off occurs during a run-through or sequence when the dog must make a turn away from the object before it and must take an object that is not an obvious choice. Call-offs can be minor, such as an obstacle to the side, or can be severe, requiring the dog to turn at a sharp angle away from the obstacle in front of it.

Call-offs, generally, appear in more advanced classes. However, the rule's interpretation is largely left up to judges, some of whom may slip in a call-off that many would consider an advanced maneuver. So, training for them now will help you even in Novice trials where a call-off may inadvertently appear. Call-offs that result in off-courses can have serious penalties. In AKC standard and UKC for example, off-courses cost points. In AKC jumpers and USDAA, a dog that goes off course is eliminated.

To train your dog on call-offs, start with refining your handling techniques. Be certain you are absolutely clear on

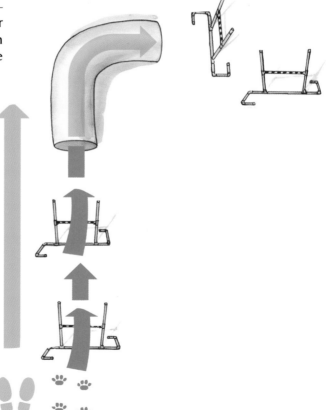

Cross-behind.

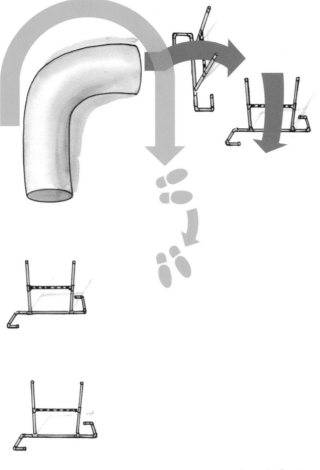

Cross-in-front.

Traps

A trap is similar to a call-off as it is intended to lure the dog off course. Unlike the call-off, the trap is less subtle. A trap is two objects side-by-side with entry points near each other. An example of a trap is an A-frame with a tunnel running underneath with its entry points next to each other. Like call-offs, traps have various degrees of difficulty.

For the beginning dog owner, traps can seem unfair. Tunnels seem to suck the novice dog right in and even experienced dogs can have trouble with them. Unclear handling will certainly cause a dog to take the wrong

Training call-offs.

obstacle. While novice courses aren't *supposed* to have traps, I've seen some courses that have something that looks remarkably like a trap, albeit a minor trap.

When approaching a trap, handle from the side where the trap obstacle is. For example, if Ace is supposed to take the tunnel on the left and the trap obstacle, the A-frame, is on the right, you too should be on the right and direct Ace to the tunnel. Your presence will somewhat block the dog's entry into the trap, plus direct the dog into the tunnel. As a beginner, you should at first do everything you can to discourage your dog from entering the trap. Later, as Ace becomes more accustomed to your commands (and you become a better handler) you can reduce the amount of blocking to very little and Ace will be focused more on your directions.

Call-off.
Ace's normal inclination is to take the tunnel (not shown) after the first jump. Call him to the second jump with a "Here!" command. Stetson, the Great Dane, and owner demonstrate.

Overhandling and Blocking

When you first start training sequencing, you may need to handle Ace more than what you will be allowed to do at a real trial. This is natural. However, as Ace becomes more accustomed to your commands and handling, you too should be refining your technique. There is nothing better than seeing good handling in the ring. Likewise, there is nothing worse than seeing someone yell, plead, and cajole their dog into doing obstacles. It looks bad to spectators and gives agility an undeserved bad reputation.

Overhandling encompasses more than the handler giving a million commands to take an obstacle (each one louder than before). It also encompasses blocking where the handler tries to prevent the dog from doing anything but the obstacle. UKC, for example, is so focused on the handler not crossing the plane of the obstacle and not blocking that you can incur handling faults quickly. I've incurred handling faults in UKC with Kiana when I went around to the end of the dog walk and waited for her. I was inadvertently blocking the exit on the dog walk, thus making it difficult for her to miss a contact (in the judge's opinion). What I couldn't explain to the judge was there was absolutely no way she would have blown a contact at the normally reduced speed she uses on the dog walk. But the judge called the handling fault and kindly explained to me afterwards the reasoning. Lesson learned.

Likewise in UKC you cannot stand in the middle and call a dog over the jumps. In the other styles you can, but it is certainly better to stand to the side of the obstacle and command the dog over. In AKC you can be faulted for overhandling by blocking weave poles.

Should you get a fault that is not apparent, ask the judge during a break what the fault was and how you could avoid it.

Blocking. Use your body to block the sight of a potential object (in this case, a tunnel, which is not shown) to prevent an off-course. Jeffrey, the Border Collie, and owner demonstrate.

Chapter 15 Problems

What causes problems in agility? If you've been reading and using the training techniques in this book faithfully, you will hopefully not have to use this chapter. However, problems can and do occur, even in the best and most competitive dogs.

First, be aware that seldom is the dog at fault. Lack of training, unclear commands, rough handling, and biological problems all can cause problems in agility training. When handling, you may be asking for something the dog is incapable of doing, doesn't understand how to do, or lacks the confidence to do. For example, you may be asking Sierra to jump when she has injured her carpal. You may be telling her to go right when she hasn't practiced that command nearly enough. Or she may have had a terrible spill off the dog walk and is afraid or nervous about using it again. It may be hot and your dog has a double coat, or it may be cold and Sierra is a Chinese Crested and is shivering.

Whatever the problem appears to be, look deeper, especially if it appears suddenly. Chronic problems in one or two areas may signal either a training or a biological problem.

Ask yourself what you are asking Sierra to do and see if perhaps you are asking something beyond her ability. Are you chronically overtime? Does she have difficulty with the physical exertion such as climbing the A-frame? Is her attention focused elsewhere?

Breed Limitations

Certain breeds excel in agility. These include, but are not exclusive to, the Golden Retriever, Border Collie, Australian Shepherd, and Shetland Sheepdog. Likewise, you will seldom see certain breeds in agility. It is certainly not because people discourage these breeds. Rather, there are certain limitations, real or perceived, by the owners of these dogs that cause them not to try agility.

Breeds you seldom see in agility include:
- Northern breeds, such as the Alaskan Malamute, the Siberian Husky, and the Samoyed. These dogs are known to be difficult to train because of their independent spirit and their apparent unreliability with commands.
- Extremely large dogs, such as the Great Dane and the Saint Bernard. (How does that dog fit in the tunnel?) These dogs are generally less fast and have a more difficult time with plank widths and tunnels.
- Unusually built dogs such as the Basset Hound, the Dachshund, and the Bulldog. Conformation is less suited for jumping and other activities required in agility.

Some breeds have limitations when it comes to agility. Large breeds like the Great Dane are generally slower and have difficulty with certain obstacles due to their size.

These generalizations may or may not fit the individual dog or a number of dogs. Likewise, I have not included all the difficult breeds (many terrier owners may point out my omission of their favorites). If you own a dog from the breeds mentioned above, keep in mind that certain breed traits may not be conducive to making an agility champion. For instance, if your sighthound bolts after a rabbit that is across the field away from the agility ring, realize that this is a breed trait. You have an uphill battle at training him to work off leash outside. Perhaps choose only agility trials that are held indoors.

Can you ever have a reliable dog from a nonstandard breed? Absolutely! I have seen dogs out of each of the breeds listed doing agility and obtaining titles, and even appearing in national competitions. Difficult breeds can do agility. If anything, the title is more of a reflection on the trainer than the dog. Difficult breeds may take longer and may require different training and handling techniques. They may require innovation on the part of the trainer.

For example, you may have noticed that I have included my favorite breed, the Alaskan Malamute, among difficult breeds. Kiana does her best in cooler weather. Since she is a Malamute, that is expected. But she also does her best when she hasn't trained agility in two or three weeks. The longer the time between training and trials, the better she performs. If I work with her too much, she becomes bored and decides that other things are much more interesting. She will think up new and exciting ways to handle an obstacle or ignore my commands. For many dogs, this time-off period doesn't work, but for her, it is the only way to get consistent performances.

• Sighthounds, such as the Greyhound, the Whippet, the Saluki, and the Borzoi. Movement easily distracts them and they may run away and chase a blowing piece of paper. They are also independent, given their hunting and coursing heritage.

Determining If the Problem Is Biological

Some problems are caused by biological or physical problems that are not necessarily apparent. Take Ace to the veterinarian for a thorough checkup if you see any of the following:

- Chronic refusals on jumps.
- Limping.
- Sudden dislike of agility training.
- Acting up in the ring to stop the training sessions.
- An overall reluctance in activities that he normally enjoys.
- Whimpering or crying when performing an obstacle.
- Loss of appetite.
- Lethargy or lack of energy.
- Obsessive licking and sucking of feet and legs (marked by reddened hair).

Even if Ace is not showing any of the above symptoms, a trip to the veterinarian might be in order if you are having training problems. Rule out the biological factors before focusing on the training problems, especially if there is no apparent cause for the current problems. For an entire year, I was convinced Kiana hated jumping. Occasionally, she would land wrong and limp, so I would have to rest her and she would seem to get better. One day, her leg started swelling. I took her to the veterinarian. My veterinarian looked at the strange growths on her legs that I thought were malformed pads. My veterinarian biopsied them and determined that these strange growths were dematomes (skin that grows inward), harmless to her health but they were irritating her legs as she jumped. We had them removed, and a year after the operation, I found Kiana loved to jump.

If you have a sudden or recurring problem, take Ace to the veterinarian for a full physical. Request that your veterinarian give Ace a thorough orthopedic exam and perhaps a blood chemistry panel or CBC. If Ace is acting lethargic or is limping, consider having a blood test done for tick-borne diseases such as Lyme. Your veterinarian may not find anything, but still do not rule out another possible undiagnosed problem.

One common problem is a dog suddenly refusing the A-frame. If this occurs, clip your dog's nails. Your dog should have shorter nails than dogs in conformation or obedience. If a dog's nails grow too long, the nails may jam into the dog's foot on impact as the dog scrambles down the A-frame. This is painful and avoidable. Keep your dog's nails cut short!

Run-outs and Refusals

A *run-out* is when the dog runs past the obstacle, causing what is termed a *refusal*. A *refusal* is when the dog either balks or hesitates before an obstacle or passes the plane of the obstacle. AKC and USDAA heavily penalize refusals. (UKC does not consider refusals to be faults unless the dog has committed to the obstacle.) There can be several reasons for run-outs and refusals including:

- Asking the dog to take an obstacle he hasn't committed to.
- Asking a dog to perform an obstacle while giving unclear signals.
- Asking the dog to perform an obstacle without enough space to perform it.

A run-out at the tire.

- Turning the dog away from the obstacle too close to the intended obstacle (handler induced refusals).
- Allowing the dog to enter the obstacle poorly.
- Asking the dog to perform an obstacle he is unsure or uneasy about.
- Asking the dog to perform an obstacle while he is lame, hot, or sick.

If you've noticed, the above reasons for refusals are all handler induced. There can be other reasons for refusals, including independent natures and boredom, but these are uncommon, whereas the above reasons are fairly common.

If you are asking Ace to perform an obstacle that he is unsure or uneasy about, it is time to go back to basics and work him on the individual obstacle until he gains (regains) his confidence. For example, let's say Ace had a bad

experience with the dog walk. Maybe he tumbled off one or the one you had been working on was rickety and it spooked him. Start working the dog walk now. Choose the widest, lowest, and most sturdy dog walk to lead him over. (Use an 8-foot walk if you can find one.) Start working Ace over the walk to gain confidence, just as though he was a dog doing this the first time. Don't pause and let him think about his predicament, just get him through. Give him lots of treats and praise. Keep focusing on that dog walk, but intersperse a few fun obstacles so you don't wear him out. End the session with a morale builder such as a favorite obstacle or a play session. End on a positive note.

Another technique is called backchaining, which works well for dogs that have had bad experiences with a piece of equipment. In the above example of Ace falling off the dog walk, you can pick up Ace (assuming Ace is not too heavy) and put him on the downside of the dog walk a foot from the end. Give him a treat and then lead him off. In this way, Ace has learned that there is a safe way to leave the obstacle. As Ace grows more confident with the obstacle, put him a little higher on the downside and then lead him off. (Don't forget your *touch* command.) As Ace's confidence builds, you can start him further up the dog walk each time until finally he is ready to enter the walk himself.

A common cause for refusals is when a dog has missed a jump and the handler brings the dog back to perform the jump and the dog balks. Often the handler has not given the dog enough room to properly commit to the jump. If Ace misses a jump due to a run-out or refusal, lead Ace farther out, giving him as much room and the best possible entrance to the jump as you can.

Missing Contacts

Dogs that miss contacts are often larger and very fast dogs. The reason the dog misses the contacts is because the handler fails to enforce the *touch, wait,* or *rest* command on the contacts. Reread Chapter 6, Teaching Contacts, to learn the proper way to rest your dog on the contacts. When you train Ace to stop at contacts, he is less likely to miss the downside of contacts.

Most dogs miss the contacts at the downside, although a few dogs will miss them on the upside, especially the A-frame with UKC. Missing contacts is a complete elimination in AKC standard, whereas other organizations severely penalize for them. In

UKC, for example, if a dog misses a contact, the judge will call "fault" and the dog has two more tries to get the contact right. This incurs points lost and time lost.

If Ace habitually misses contacts, start slowing him down once he commits to the obstacle and right before the end contact. At this point, accuracy is more important than lost time—all that speed doesn't do you any good if you're NQ'd for a missed contact.

Knocked Down Bars

Knocked down bars can NQ a run or cause a severe penalty. First, consider if Ace is getting enough room to lead into the jump. Many big dogs require more room to land from a jump and run up to a jump than smaller dogs. If Ace needs more room between jumps, make your own, if necessary, to give him a good running start at a jump.

If your dog does not know how to jump properly, reread Chapter 7, and work on jumps. Practice at lower heights and gradually introduce the dog to higher levels. If your dog has trouble jumping the regulation height, have your veterinarian check Ace out thoroughly.

Dogs that consistently knock down bars may not realize they knock down bars, especially if the dog is big. You can take the PVC pipe jump bar, fill it with sand, and cap it on both ends. When your larger dog jumps and hits the bar with his toes or tail, he will feel something weighty and will hear the louder drop. Whenever Ace knocks down a bar, put him in a down-stay and put the bar back in place. The pause in the fun will signal something happened and that he should pay attention to it.

Acting Up in the Ring

Dogs act up in the ring for a variety of reasons. By acting up, I mean that the dog is behaving wildly and uncontrollable. I've had one experience with acting up with Kiana, and believe me, it was one experience too many. We were at the second day of our first trial. Everything started normally with two jumps and then Kiana saw the tunnel. She ran through the tunnel and as I called her back, she went over the A-frame. Then she went through the tunnel and to the top of the A-frame and wagged her head at the crowd with a demonically pleased look on her face. The crowd was in stitches.

Acting up can happen at any time and to any dog, regardless of the experience. I've seen dogs in Open classes act as uncontrollable as rank novices have.

TIP: Attend as Many Different Training Classes as Possible

Attend different training classes in different locations, using different equipment. It will get Ace used to a variety of different places, smells, and noises, plus different-looking equipment. For example, some clubs or training facilities may only have 8-foot (2.4 m) dog walks (due to space), whereas in a trial or another facility you may use a 12-foot (3.7 m) dog walk. Some training facilities have plain jumps, whereas some may have unusual silhouettes. Desensitize Ace by getting him used to going to different places and experiencing different equipment.

The most common reasons for acting up are:
- The dog enjoys the attention and audience response.
- The dog has become "ring-wise" and knows you cannot correct him at a trial.
- The dog hates the trial, or an obstacle within the run-through. Uses the behavior to get out of doing the trial.
- The dog is very new at trials and is overwhelmed by the crowds and attention.
- The dog senses the handler's stress and become stressed.

Don't feel badly if Ace agile dog starts acting like Ace Idiot. Just realize you must solve this problem NOW before it becomes a habit. Determining why Ace is doing this will be the key to eliminating this problem and focusing on agility.

The Show Off Who Is "Ring-Wise"

Many dogs start acting up in the trial ring because they did so once and the crowd reinforced the behavior. They are big hams at heart and enjoy being the center of attention. He's become ring-wise because he knows you can't correct him in the ring—you can't touch him if you want to finish the run. This behavior becomes more enforced as the dog hears the delighted laughter. Unfortunately, you can't stop the audience from chuckling. You can, however, take the reinforcement away from him the moment he starts misbehaving. And regardless of what Ace Idiot thinks, you can correct him. The fun ends immediately, causing a bigger correction.

When Ace starts to misbehave in the ring, stop everything. Ask the judge to be excused. If Ace is acting wild but hasn't lost all sense of intelligence, he will most likely respond to a *Here!* command, if you've been training with food. Hold your hand out as though you have a piece of food and wait for Ace to come and take it. If you can't catch Ace, see if you can put him in a down-stay. Don't chase him all over the agility ring, screaming and yelling as this might cause him to leave the ring. Remember he is too fast for you to catch him while running, but do whatever you can to stop the behavior. Once you catch him, calmly, quietly, take him out of the ring. Don't give him a treat. Don't praise or reward him. Just leave and put him in his crate and ignore him for a while.

Some dogs will automatically exit the ring. Have a friend or someone outside the ring lure him over with food and catch him. Again, don't chase him—many dogs will run if chased. If he comes to you, give him the food. Don't punish him or you'll risk never catching him again if he acts up. Tell him he is a good dog for coming and bring him to his crate.

Once the agility run and the fun has been taken away, most dogs when crated will sit and ponder this. This correction works for dogs that are acting up because they enjoy agility and have discovered a newfound freedom. Ace may not make the connection the first few times, but if you are consistent, he will learn that acting up means sitting in the crate and not having any fun.

The Trial-Hater or the Show-Off that Doesn't Make the Connection

Some dogs, however, don't make the connection between leaving the ring and bad behavior or perhaps they act up because they hate the trial and want a good excuse to

Many problems can be avoided through consistent training. Xena, the Bulldog, has no problems with the chute tunnel.

get out. In the latter case, you'll be doing exactly what Ace wants you to do—getting him out of what he considers an odious task.

The first step to changing this behavior is to find something that motivates Ace—a special toy, a game you play, a certain type of food, or anything that Ace loves, and use it only in agility or during trials. So, if Ace goes wild over fried chicken, make a special stop before the trial at the local chicken fast food restaurant and purchase some boneless fried chicken nuggets. If there is a park next to the trial, go to the park and work on jumping, *here,* and *get out.* Bring a favorite toy and play fetch. Reward Ace with fried chicken. Put him in a good mood so when you do go into the ring, he may be thinking fried chicken.

The other thing you can do is *correct* the behavior. If there are agility fun matches in your area, use the fun match as a training tool. A fun match is often run like a trial and there are many strange dogs present, so it gives you the opportunity to train under trial conditions. Most fun matches are lax enough to allow leashes, food, and other training devices in the ring, unless they are AKC sanctioned matches. Some matches do placements, but if you talk to the judge and tell her that this is only a training exercise and you don't want a placement, she may let you train in the ring. Whichever match you attend, be certain to tell the judge your problem and tell her of your strategy for how you are going to handle it. Most are willing to help if you keep them informed.

Put two leashes on Ace, his regular leash and either a tab, light long line, or what obedience trainers call a shark line. (A shark line is a very thin line made from thin wire that has a T at the end for you to hold.) When Ace decides to act up, you have a method of reeling him back in and having him finish the course on leash.

Start by removing the regular leash, making sure Ace is aware that you removed it. Now, start the run as you would, making sure that Ace doesn't catch the long line or shark line on any equipment. (If you use a tab, it will be easier.) When Ace begins to misbehave, grasp the line and gently reel him towards you with a *Here!* Now that you have his attention, finish the course, with him on leash! Praise and treat him.

Now, you've given Ace something to think about. If you've never before done this to him and he had been acting up in the ring, now he's going to think this might happen again. If you have the chance, do another run through or attend another fun

match and set him up in the same way. A few of these short lessons and Ace will be convinced you *can* correct him in the ring and make him finish the course.

The Dog that Has Had a Bad Experience

Inevitably, Ace may have a bad experience with an obstacle in the trial ring. He may tumble off the dog walk or A-frame, get caught in the chute, or bump himself with the teeter. It may be something as innocuous as a wobbly table or strange looking jump wings that scared him. Regardless of the reason, it has become a bad experience.

First, as heartless as this sounds, don't show much sympathy. Dogs are quick to pick up emotions that reinforce their behavior. Unless Ace is injured, don't fawn over him and don't cuddle and praise him. If you do, you've just enforced the behavior he exhibited. Act as though nothing happened and continue onward. Allow him to shake it off, give him a hearty pat, and continue. Usually nothing will come of that if you act like it wasn't a big deal.

If you have the chance, practice on the piece of equipment that gave him trouble before the next trial. For example, if Ace got caught in the chute in the trial on Saturday morning, work with him and the chute Saturday evening in training class, so Ace will be ready for the chute on Sunday. Have a few good runs and then end the training session on a positive note. Ace will be more inclined to shrug off the bad experience.

Suppose you didn't shrug it off or Ace has reacted badly to the obstacle, regardless of what you are doing. You've tried training him on the same obstacle in agility classes and he is still fearful. Try training him on obstacles he isn't afraid of and then give him some rest time. A few weeks or a month of not doing agility may give him enough distance between the bad experience. Don't enter any more trials or matches at this time. Another bout of bad behavior will continue to cement the behavior. After the rest period, begin retraining him on the obstacle, always ending on a positive note. End the session training on obstacles that Ace enjoys or play with him a while.

Once you are certain that Ace is confident with the obstacle, attend a fun match and try him out. If the judge allows you to correct, use a leash, or use food in the fun match, do it. Watch for possible backsliding towards the fearful behavior and work through it. The fun match may show that you need more work or may show that Ace is ready for trials again. Whatever you do, don't rush him through the training. Some dogs need time to get beyond a bad experience.

Kiana is the type of dog that sours easily with too much training. By taking time off and giving her a fresh perspective after several months off, she became more competitive and earned two titles in a summer. She forgot most of her bad habits and focused on the training. I discovered this by accident, after taking the winter off to pursue other things. In the springtime, we were able to complete her UKC title and obtain two legs towards her AKC NA. Her title came in early September after a month off.

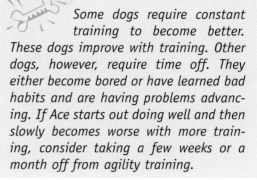

TIP: Taking Time Off

Some dogs require constant training to become better. These dogs improve with training. Other dogs, however, require time off. They either become bored or have learned bad habits and are having problems advancing. If Ace starts out doing well and then slowly becomes worse with more training, consider taking a few weeks or a month off from agility training.

run-through sequence. This can disqualify runs in AKC Jumpers, NADAC, and USDAA classes. As a handler, you must be clear in your commands. Practice traps and call-offs until your handling and Ace's responsiveness makes you both reliable. Many off courses are due to poor handling.

Do not teach Ace to jump over the same hurdle backwards unless you command him to. That is an easy way to obtain an off-course penalty. A familiar scenario follows: dog misses a jump, handler calls the dog back, the dog takes the jump backwards, causing a refusal and an off-course penalty. If Ace runs out on a jump, go to the side *away* from the jump and call Ace to you. You don't need to worsen the refusal with an off course.

Making Agility Fun

With all the training and focus on perfect runs, never forget to have fun. Sometimes our competitive nature gets the best of us and we forget why we are doing agility. If you are doing agility simply for the titles and ribbons, choose something else—don't

Off Courses

An off course is where the dog takes an obstacle or obstacles that are not in the

Clicker Training

Clicker training is a form of operant conditioning where you train the dog to expect food after hearing the sound of the click. There is no negative reinforcement, other than no clicks and treats. You train the dog by clicking and then rewarding the treat. The time between the click and the treat can be long or short.

When the dog does something right, such as a pause at a contact, the trainer clicks the clicker at the moment the behavior is exhibited, thus enforcing the behavior. The dog receives the treat after the click. Clicker training is helpful in enforcing exact behavior as you can click at the precise moment what you wish the dog to do.

After the dog exhibits the behavior, you can use a cue word, such as *touch,* before the behavior, then a click, and then a treat. Eventually, you can use a word such as *Good!* with the click and phase out the clicks, using the word *Good!* as the signal.

Clickers and other training devices are not allowed in trials, but it does not mean you cannot use them during training sessions to enforce good behavior. The good behavior becomes a habit rather than an exception, and you will quickly find you don't need a clicker to have an excellent performance. Plus, you can always click *after* a run and treat the dog.

For more information concerning clicker training, read Karen Pryor's *Don't Shoot the Dog!* and *Clicker Training for Dogs.* (See Appendix B—Agility References, page 201).

drag your dog along for the ride. Ace will disappoint you eventually, because he is a dog. If you aren't having fun and he isn't having fun, then perhaps you shouldn't be doing agility. Of course, winning titles and ribbons is more fun than another NQ, but you should be keeping a sense of humor and realize that dogs are not push-button animals.

Ace will do stupid things. So will you. Ace may get bored with training. You might too. Start making agility fun by playing games with him. If he enjoys a game of fetch, tag, or whatever, start or end your training sessions with a game. If he likes a toy filled with treats or a long romp in the park, give it to him. Sometimes fun matches include agility games, such as tunnel pretzels or weave pole knockouts. Use these games as a way to have fun and not to insist on perfection.

Play training and clicker training are popular now because they provide other positive reinforcement techniques. Use these methods in conjunction with your current training; you might stumble across a training technique both of you will enjoy. These methods can only help promote new interest in training.

If you are constantly negative, Ace will not enjoy agility, and you will eventually have poor performances. If you are positive and upbeat, Ace will enjoy agility and work harder towards pleasing you.

Chapter 16
Competition

Competition or Just for Fun?

Most of this book assumes you'll be preparing for competition. Training as though you were competing will make you a better handler and Sierra a well-trained dog even if you never intend to enter a trial.

However, there are many good reasons to stay away from competition. Such reasons include:

- Expense. Competition can be expensive, costing anywhere from $13 to $40 per trial.
- Competition focuses on points, scores, and perfect runs, not necessarily on having fun.
- It's easy to become disappointed in your dog because of a missed contact or knocked down bar.

But competition can be fun. Where else would you be able to compare yourself and your dog against other teams and still come out a winner? Everyone has a chance at qualifying and earning a leg towards his or her dog's title. If Sierra does well, she can also win a placement—that is, a first through fourth place ribbon. Each jump height has placements, so each qualifier has a chance at placing. (In NADAC, you don't even have to qualify to have a placement ribbon!)

TIP: Trial Premium List

Before you can sign up for a trial, you must obtain a trial premium list. Within the premium is the information listing for the trial including dates and times, entry limitations (if any), entry closure, certification (by agility organization), trial hours and location, judges, entry fees, awards, class information, height divisions, and entry forms. You can find out about local trials by contacting the national organizations (see appendices for web addresses and phone numbers), local kennel clubs, or dog trainers. Once you have attended one or two trials, you are usually put on the mailing list for most trials in your area.

Be certain to enter early. In some metropolitan areas, trials fill up fast and reach their limit. Sometimes this occurs within a day or two. Most trials have a closing date for entries within the premium (usually on the first page). A few trials will accept walk-ins, but this is rare.

Matches seldom have premiums, but some clubs hold matches so they can obtain AKC certification for trials in the next year. These matches are run just like trials. Fun matches usually do not require premiums or advanced registration and are usually less formal.

Competition also allows you to compare your progress with others. You can watch top-notch teams in excellent and open classes and learn techniques you might not otherwise see. As you start attending more trials, you'll start recognizing faces and enjoy cheering on people and dogs whom you've met at other trials.

Which Trials or Matches to Enter?

Most of your entries may have to do with the availability of trials in your area. For example, if breed clubs in your area hold AKC events, chances are you are going to participate in AKC trials. Some geographic areas may only have USDAA. If you are lucky enough to have a choice, choose the trials and matches that suit your dog and your handling. For example, in Colorado, USDAA and AKC trials are prevalent. However, UKC has three or four trial weekends throughout the year, enabling handlers and dogs to earn titles. NADAC, on the other hand, has only one trial weekend per year. I've chosen AKC and UKC competition as they are less fast-paced than USDAA and NADAC, plus they have enough trials within the area to earn a title.

If you live near a major metropolitan area, chances are there is more than one agility style available. USDAA and NADAC are fast-paced and highly competitive. AKC is quite popular but does not allow mixed breeds in competition. UKC has more emphasis on handling and longer times. Your dog's speed and the trial availability in your area may limit your choices.

This Golden Retriever enjoys jumping over this panel jump.

Where Trials Are Held

Trials are held either indoors or outside. Unlike a conformation or obedience show, agility requires larger rings and may have one or two rings. Agility trials are often held in county fairgrounds, in public parks, on college campuses, or in horse barns—anyplace where there is a large enough flat area to handle a large ring and associated trial goers and dogs, spectators, and equipment. Sometimes, if a conformation show is at a site large enough, the kennel club may host an agility trial as well. You may see AKC or UKC shows with agility trials.

Which is better, indoors or outdoors? The obvious benefit to having a trial indoors is that the trial goers are more or less protected from inclement weather. There is less chance of a dog escaping. However, if the building is not air conditioned, an indoor arena can become stifling hot in the summertime. Horse barns and arenas can provide distractions, especially if the stable is nearby and your dog is not familiar with horses. Many dogs find horse droppings and other items left in horse arenas to be a delicacy—something that you don't need in your dog's diet! Also, unless the floor is dirt, most indoor floors are hard on the dog's joints. Concrete provides no cushion. Even with mats, a dog can slip and injure itself. PA systems can spook a dog unused to them.

Outdoors can be pleasant or an ordeal, depending on the weather. Without shade, dogs can overheat quickly in the summertime. If it rains, the grass and obstacles become slippery and a dog can easily injure himself. Likewise, once wet, the chute

TIP: How to Register

If this is your first time competing, you will most likely be running in the beginning or novice class. This is Standard Novice in AKC, AG-I in UKC, Novice Standard in NADAC, and Starters or Novice in USDAA. Some organizations differentiate between experienced handlers and inexperienced handlers. Novice A is the class where those handlers run who have never put an agility title on a dog. Novice B is for those who have put agility titles on a dog before. If you have put an agility title on a dog in any style of agility, you must run in the Novice B class. The only exception to this rule is AKC, which does not recognize titles from other styles. Hence, someone who has obtained titles on their dogs in USDAA only must run in the Novice A class in AKC.

You can enter other classes as a novice. In AKC, you can enter Novice Jumpers with Weaves. In UKC, you can enter both AG-I and AG-II simultaneously.

becomes difficult for small dogs to push their way through. A misstep along uneven ground can cause a twisted shoulder. A dog that is easily distracted or unreliable off leash may run away, especially if there is no fencing. But, running outdoors is fun and can be a wonderful experience if the weather cooperates.

If Sierra is reliable off leash, consider attending either indoors or outdoors trials. If Sierra is easily distracted, it might be better to go to an indoor trial. (Even then, many indoor trials keep the doors open for ventilation.) The trial facilities are listed in

What to Bring to a Trial or Match

- Water (for both you and your dog)
- Dog bowls
- Umbrella and rain gear
- Pavilion or sun shade
- Wide-brimmed hat
- Cooler with snacks or lunch, soda pop, sports drink
- Folding chair
- Crate (collapsible crates work well if your dog won't chew through them) and crate caddy
- Portable battery-operated fan (hot weather)
- Blankets (cold weather)
- Sweater or jacket (cold weather)
- Mat to set crate on
- First aid kit
- Premium list and running order
- Leashes
- Dog treats
- Dog food
- Dog toys
- Cash
- Poop bags
- Collar without tags
- Rule book

the premium including whether the trial is held indoors or outdoors. If the trial is held outdoors, it will go on, regardless of the weather, so be prepared.

On the Road with Fido

Sometimes trials are farther away than a few hours' drive and require that you spend the night in a different town. If this is your first trial, try to attend a local trial, rather than

put Sierra through the stress of traveling as well as the stress of a trial. However, traveling may be unavoidable, especially if you live in a rural area or it is very difficult to travel short distances without spending hours on the road due to traffic.

Pre-travel Preparations

Now is a good time to make certain Sierra has all her vaccinations and is up-to-date on her heartworm medication. Sierra should be vaccinated against distemper, parvovirus, coronavirus, kennel cough (infectious tracheobronchitis), and other infectious diseases with a 7-way or 8-way vaccine. Dog shows are notorious for spreading contagious diseases such as kennel cough, parvovirus, and minor intestinal disorders. Even though most breeders and dog show entrants vaccinate their dogs and take precautions, the constant exposure to a large number of entrants that travel frequently increases the probability of infection.

If you are traveling by car, be certain your vehicle is in good running order. Have it tuned up and inspected for any possible failures. Both the heater and air conditioner should be in good working order. Purchase a travel crate in which your dog can lay comfortably in. Purchase a small stainless steel bucket and a double snap. Attach it to the crate's inside door and fill it halfway with water. (Don't use the little plastic airline dishes—dogs find them delicious). If the weather is hot, you can purchase a small battery-operated fan that attaches to the crate and will ventilate it.

If you are traveling by plane, Sierra will need a health certificate. All airlines require a health certificate before shipping a dog. Your veterinarian can provide the certificate

A Golden Retriever deftly jumps the double bar hurdle in a trial.

for a fee. Sierra will need all her vaccinations up-to-date as well. Schedule the health certificate within 10 days of travel. When you book your flight, be certain that the airline knows you will have a dog with you. You must transport Sierra in an FAA approved kennel with stickers saying "live animals" along the side and top. Choose only direct flights with no layovers and check with the airline first before shipping a dog during hot or cold weather.

Dogs must have a water and food bowl available to them. If you use the plastic clip-on type cups, be sure Sierra is not a chewer. Otherwise, purchase stainless steel cups that can clip inside. Purchase a plastic page protector and affix it to the top of Sierra's crate. Write a quick note to the airlines stating clearly your destination, phone numbers, your home address, and the phone numbers of your veterinarians. Include the health certificate and instructions for feeding and watering. Tape the page protector shut and attach a small package of dog food to the crate as well. I also use a permanent marker to write my home address and telephone number on the crate.

> ### TIP: Dress for Comfort, Not for Success
>
> *Unlike other dog shows, the rule for agility is comfort. Everything you wear should keep you comfortable, should it be cold or hot. Wear shorts and a cool shirt in the summer; jeans and sweatshirts in the winter. Just don't wear tank tops or cut-offs.*

TIP: Agility Collar or Running Naked?

USDAA and NADAC require that the dog run naked, that is, without a collar. UKC requires a dog to wear a flat buckle collar and AKC allows either. The collar must be free of all attachments. This includes hanging tags and riveted tags or tabs. Buckles and loops for the leash are OK if they are part of the collar, but you may not have a tab, leash, or other attachment that was not part of the flat collar. The only problem with running without a collar is if you have to grasp the dog quickly. The collar makes a nice handhold.

I use a special flat collar that I call Kiana's agility collar. I attach it to the dog supply bag or water bucket that I take to agility trials so I will not forget it.

Finding a Hotel or Motel

Many premium lists contain listings of hotels and motels that accept dogs. If the premium list does not, contact the trial secretary directly for information. If he or she is unable to help you, ask what hotels or motels are in the area and do some calling. Hotels vary, even among national chains, as to whether or not they accept dogs. If a place you contact does not accept dogs, don't make a reservation and try to sneak her in. Trust me, the establishment will know and you will do greater harm for all dogs and their owners by doing so. Some establishments require a damage deposit or a daily extra payment. Some have size restrictions, such as no pets over 25 pounds (11.2 kg). Whatever the rules are, abide by them.

Good Manners

Always show good manners with your dog whenever you travel. Sadly, many people abuse their welcome and now hotels and motels that once accepted dogs do not any longer. Always be mindful of the hotel's hospitality. The following are good rules for traveling:

- Always inform the hotel/motel that you have a dog.
- Never leave your dog alone in your room. A crated dog may howl or bark and disturb guests. A loose dog may destroy things or soil the carpet.
- Ask the front desk where you can exercise your dog. Bring a plastic bag or pooper scoop and pick up feces.
- Never leave your dog in a car in warm weather during the daytime, even with the windows cracked. Cars heat up quickly and your dog can suffer heat stroke.
- Don't bathe, brush, or groom your dog in a hotel room.
- Don't let your dog sleep in the bed with you. (The next person may not like dog hair on the blankets and bedspread.)
- Put your dog's dishes in the bathroom or any place where there is a tiled or linoleum floor. Dogs sometimes spill food and water when eating or drinking.
- Do not let your dog off leash to run.
- Keep your dog quiet.
- Use a lint brush or dog hair roller to remove any dog hair from the furniture and carpet.
- Leave the room in good shape.
   Checklist for overnight items
- Dog food (enough for several days)
- Extra poop bags
- Trash bags
- Veterinary medicine

- Vaccination records
- Health records
- Sturdy travel crate
- Cellular phone
- Maps
- Enzymatic cleaning solution for accidents
- Lint brush or dog fur tape roller (sold in pet supply stores to remove pet hair from clothes)

What to Expect at Your First Trial or Match

You've registered Sierra for the trial. Most trials will send you registration confirmation and a schedule of the running order. Registration time is very important. Most registration times are early so you have enough time to get settled in and watch some of the other classes going on. Set up your crate and belongings in an area where Sierra will be most comfortable. Trials are stressful to many dogs. If all the activity overwhelms Sierra, put her in a crate in a quiet place. If Sierra gets anxious if you're out of sight, put her crate in a place where she can see you at any time. Kiana gets extremely agitated if she cannot see me and may try to chew through the crate. I will either have her with me or will put her crate in a place where she can watch me even from the other side of the arena.

Once you arrive and set up your equipment, you should look for the registration table and check in. At the registration table, you will receive an armband or sticker with your dog's name and your number. If you

A Golden Retriever clears the triple bar jump.

Tip: Show Etiquette

The following are the rules for behavior (both written and unwritten) at an agility trial:

- *Bring plastic bags and clean up after Sierra when she defecates.*
- *Keep Sierra on leash or in a crate, under control at all times.*
- *No slip collars in the ring at any time. (USDAA allows a slip collar or lead, but it must be removed before the dog begins its run; no training collars of any type.) No prong or pinch collars on show grounds.*
- *Do not touch someone else's dog without his or her permission first.*
- *Do not allow Sierra to approach another dog without first asking the owner. This includes sniffing, playing, and other possible contact. Many dogs are intolerant of strange dogs and you could have a fight on your hands that would be your fault.*
- *No food, toys, or training devices in the ring at a trial at any time. If this is a fun match, ask the judge if you are allowed to use food or training items.*
- *If, for whatever reason, you must cut your run short (e.g., because of an out-of-control dog), ask the judge to be excused first. (Be polite.)*
- *Be at the ring early. Check in with the gate steward.*
- *Don't talk badly about another competitor. Don't loudly analyze a dog's performance while in the ring.*
- *Be sensitive to people's feelings. Don't tell them, "Boy, your dog was an idiot today." Use common sense.*
- *Don't take up more room than you absolutely need. Crating areas may be in short supply and you may have to share. Likewise, be sensitive to people's space. Don't put your tent or crate directly in front of other people's tents or crates.*
- *Don't change the bar on the practice jump without seeing who is waiting to use it. If the 24-inch class is next in competition and you have a 12-inch dog, let those with 24-inch dogs practice first.*

have multiple dogs or are running in multiple classes, such as standard and jumpers with weaves, you will receive an armband or sticker for each dog and each class. If you receive a sticker, you can wear it on your shirt or sleeve—it doesn't matter. You may also receive a diagram with the course layout you will be running. If you are not provided with a course layout, look for a posting board displaying the course. Spend some time studying the layout to determine the best way to handle Sierra. You will also receive the actual running order for dogs, which includes the dog's name and breed, so you can keep track of who is ahead of you.

You may notice that within the Novice class, there is a Novice A and a Novice B. (Within USDAA there is a Starters and a Novice class.) Usually Novice B goes before Novice A (Novice precedes Starters in USDAA.) If you are in Novice A (Starters), your placement will be judged against other Novice A (Starters) participants in your height class, so you are not judged against those who have previously earned titles.

Depending on when you arrived, use any extra time you have to walk Sierra so she can relieve herself, warm her up, practice jumps (there is a practice hurdle available to you), and play with her so she won't be stressed out. Warming up Sierra is important! Dogs do not warm up by themselves, so you will have to warm her up. Good warm-up exercises include walking/jogging her around, playing fetch, and jumping her over the practice hurdle. You can judge when the Novice classes will begin by multiplying the number of entries by approximately 1½ minutes. This should include course changes, awards, and height changes, but does not account for no-shows. This gives you only an estimate, so be aware that it could be way off.

In all styles of agility, you will have a judge's briefing and a walkthrough. In AKC, you will have a contact familiarization time where you can walk your dog over the contacts once. In UKC, dogs have course familiarization, meaning they can actually perform the course once on leash.

It is up to the judge in what order the judge's briefing, the walkthrough, and the contact familiarization occurs.

The Walkthrough

The walkthrough is where you will walk the course without your dog. Before you start your walkthrough, put Sierra in her crate or ask someone to hold her while you walk the course. Now is the time for you to look at the obstacles and the course layout and determine your strategy. Walkthroughs will often solidify plans that you've been unsure about or change plans entirely. Looking at the course on a map and planning your strategy is one thing, but being out on the course is another. The obstacles will be numbered, usually with bright orange cones. Follow the cones and the map to determine your course.

Watch other competitors to see what line they are following. While you know your dog best and know what will work for you, sometimes experienced handlers might give you a fresh perspective on how you might handle part of the course. You have ten minutes or more to walk the course—use the time to consider all options and settle on what feels right for you and your dog. Don't discount other plans, but don't be persuaded to handle a certain way because "everybody else is doing it." Your dog may be used to a different style than theirs or may require different handling. Let's say you have a small dog—an 8-incher. You certainly aren't going to handle the same way as someone with a 24-inch dog.

Once you have finalized your plans, consider running through the entire course (of course, without your dog!) to get a feel for how it will work when you are out there with Sierra. The run should feel natural or, at least, flowing. If it doesn't, try something different in those sections that don't flow. Eventually, you will be so tired of walking the course or the stewards will call time, that you will leave the course.

Use the walkthrough and the contact familiarization to check out the equipment. I routinely check out the dog walk, table, and A-frame for sturdiness. Sometimes the table will be set up wobbly or the A-frame might not be set up correctly. If you find a problem with any of the equipment, alert the judge and make sure it is corrected before the trial starts.

An agility trial walkthrough.

Watching the walkthrough can be amusing. Some people talk to the air as if commanding an invisible dog. Some people actually correct their invisible dog. Somehow, the words seem to cement their actions.

The Contact Familiarization (AKC)

In the contact familiarization, you may take Sierra over the teeter, the A-frame, and the dog walk *once*. You can do this on or off leash, but I recommend on leash because of the large numbers of dogs. This allows the novice dog a chance to experience an unfamiliar surface and to determine if there might be a potential problem with the equipment. Dogs see color poorly—they can see colors somewhat but they look dim or washed out. The only refusals I've

ever had with Kiana on all three contact obstacles were at the same trial where the obstacles were painted light blue and light yellow. I have never seen a refusal like this before or since. My guess is she could not discern the obstacles until right before she had to perform them.

You can use the contact familiarization to enforce contacts or do some minor training in the ring (such as *touch*); however, if Sierra bails off the contact obstacle early or performs it poorly, you must move on. AKC does not allow two contacts in sequence, so you cannot do any sequence training at this time.

During the contact familiarization, you cannot lead Sierra through or over any other obstacles. You cannot walk her through the course. If there are more than two trials in a row, the judge may opt to skip the contact familiarization for those who attended the first day.

Course Familiarization in UKC

UKC allows you to run the course once before the trial while your dog is on lead. This gives the dog the advantage of seeing the course once and performing better. It also enables you to get used to strange equipment such as the crawl tunnel, swing plank, and sway bridge in UKC.

The Judge's Briefing

The judge's briefing will be your chance to hear rules pertaining to this particular style of agility, such as the "Four Paw Rule" in AKC and USDAA. The judge will also give you course times, that is, the time you must meet or beat in order to not accrue time faults, and whether the pause table requires a sit or down. (USDAA always requires a down. In UKC AGI, you can choose sit or down, but you must stay with it once you have given the command.) If you have any questions concerning the course, now is the time to ask. Don't feel foolish asking questions, the judge has heard it all before and no question is stupid. Ask for clarification if you don't understand something.

Your Run-through

As you're waiting for your run, no doubt you will be nervous. Try to relax and enjoy it. No matter what you do, no matter how good or bad you perform, the run will be over in less than a minute and a half.

Contact familiarization.

Remove the leash (and collar if it has tags) and hand it to the steward. Most judges prefer the next dog on the starting line when the other dog is halfway through the course. That is usually when the dog on the course leaves the table.

Start with enough room before the start line. If you touch your dog after she crosses the start line, you will be disqualified (in USDAA, you will be faulted). You can lightly hold your dog by the collar and let go before the start line. Avoid "bowling" your dog over the start line. The time starts when the dog crosses the start line.

The judge will use hand signals for scoring. A closed hand in the air indicates a refusal. An open hand in the air indicates an off-course in AKC and UKC and indicates a standard fault in USDAA. Two hands raised indicate a disqualification in AKC and UKC

and a 20-point fault in USDAA. If the judge makes a T with both hands or holds up two fingers, that indicates a table fault in AKC. A whistle is an indication that you should stop what you are doing and listen to the judge. It may indicate overtime. It may indicate a problem with the timer and the need to reset the time. It may indicate that you touched your dog (intentionally or inadvertently). Most whistles are bad, but regardless of what you think it means, look to the judge for guidance.

Possible situations in the ring include:
- Having trouble with an obstacle while in the ring. If Sierra refuses multiple times, you most likely have a nonqualifying run. Continue to try to coax Sierra to perform the obstacle, if you want; otherwise, continue, take the NQ for failure to perform, and finish the course. The judge may

A Golden Retriever tips the teeter at a trial.

request that you go on after many failed attempts.

- Getting lost on the course. Stop and look for the numbers on the cones. While the judge cannot tell you where to go next, a particularly nice judge may glance over at where you were supposed to go. Don't be embarrassed. Many people take the wrong course.
- Touching your dog. At no time before you cross the finish line can you touch your dog. If you do, you may be whistled off or faulted. Obviously, the exception is a dog that fell and suffered an injury or an out of control dog. Politely ask the judge to be excused and take your dog and walk off.
- Defecating and urinating in the ring. Even the most experienced dogs may do this if they suddenly become frightened or have diarrhea. Otherwise, you should have exercised your dog beforehand. You will be excused if your dog fouls the ring.
- Faults. In UKC, the judge will call fault for handling faults, missed contacts, and other problems. You may perform the obstacle again up to three times.
- Harsh commands. Keep your commands positive and upbeat. Some judges will penalize if the handler is too harsh.
- The table. Be certain to leave the table after the judge says *Go!* If your dog leaves during the count, you must put the dog back up on the table and the judge will restart the count. Leaving between the words *one* and *go* will incur a table fault.
- Excessive refusals or off courses. Do not quit or give up if you think you've missed a contact or passed the number of refusals, off-courses, or other point deductions allowed. Some judges may not have seen the missed contact or considered a refusal borderline, so your run might still be quali-

fying. Even if the run is nonqualifying, use this run as a training or learning experience.

Regardless of how Sierra performed on her first run, praise her the moment she steps across the finish line. Give her a treat and make a huge fuss over her.

Nonstandard Classes

Nonstandard classes provide variety and interest to both you and Sierra. AKC, NADAC, and USDAA offer nonstandard classes that enable the handler and dog to demonstrate their speed and abilities. AKC offers a Jumpers with Weaves class. NADAC offers a Jumpers and Gamblers class for all ability levels. USDAA offers a Jumpers, Gamblers, Relay, and Snooker Class, at all levels of Championship and Performance

---

TIP: Food in the Ring

At no time may you bring treats, toys, training devices, or food in the ring. Empty all pockets of food, leave bait bags behind, and stow away clickers before you enter the ring for contact familiarization, walk-throughs, and the trial run-through. However, this does not mean you cannot treat your dog. Most handlers have treats and food on them right up until it is time to go into the ring, thereby having a food scent on them when they enter the ring. They will also leave treats on a table, chair, or crate for when their dog has finished the run. NADAC requires no food or training devices within ten feet of the ring.

Programs, but a dog can only achieve a title at the Master's and Performance III levels. UKC does not offer a nonstandard class, per se, but offer different equipment in Agility I versus Agility II.

Jumpers or Jumpers with Weaves Class

The Jumpers Class is the most common class among all the national agility organizations. The Jumpers Class is fast paced; dogs competing will perform on hurdles, tunnels, and weave poles. There are no table or contact obstacles, hence there are faster course times. AKC, NADAC, and USDAA offer some form of a Jumpers Class.

Gambler's Class

The next common class is the Gambler's Class. The Gambler's Class starts where each obstacle is assigned a point value. The slower the obstacle, the higher the points. The handler must choose a path within the allotted time that gives her the maximum amounts of points. At the end of the timed period, the pair must perform a "gamble"—a sequence of pre-chosen obstacles—within a certain amount of time with the handler working from a distance. NADAC and USDAA offer a Gambler's Class.

Relay Class

As the name implies, the Relay Class allows multiple handlers and dogs to compete together as a team against other teams in a relay race. There are Relay Pairs (two dogs and two handlers) and Relay Teams (three or more dogs and handlers). Each dog and handler must perform the course and hand off the baton to the next dog and handler in the team. USDAA offers a Relay Class title at its Master's/Performance III level. USDAA does not offer Pairs in the Performance program.

Snooker Class

The Snooker Class is an unusual class where the handler and dog must perform the obstacles (set up in a standard or modified snooker configuration) according to a particular color pattern. The opening Snooker sequence begins where the handler must direct her dog through the obstacles in a "red-color-red-color-red-color" pattern where the color is any color object the handler chooses. Each color object has a different point value. Once the handler and dog complete the opening sequence, they finish with the closing sequence of "yellow-green-brown-blue-pink-black." USDAA offers a Snooker Class at its Master's/Performance III level.

17
National Agility
Trial Rules

Each national organization has its own standard for agility competition. While there may be similarities between the different standards, you should study each standard individually. Do not assume that because the style is similar that judging is similar. Likewise, the sport of agility is relatively new. Standards change constantly, so use this section as a guideline only. Obtain the latest standards from the organization you plan to compete in.

AKC

The Classes

AKC has two classes: Standard and Jumpers with Weaves. The Standard classes have all the AKC agility equipment with the exception of weave poles in Standard Novice class. The Jumpers with Weaves classes have weave poles, jumps, and tunnels, but no table and contact obstacles. As you might expect, the Jumpers classes are faster than the standard classes.

In Novice and Excellent classes, there is an A and B class. Novice A class is for those handlers who have never put an agility title

on their dog. Novice B class is for those who have a Novice level dog, but have put titles on their dogs previously. Excellent A is for those dogs who have not yet earned their AX or AXJ titles. Excellent B is for an AX or AXJ dog that is working on its MX, MXJ, or MACH titles.

TIP: Collars or Running Naked?

Each national agility organization has its own rules regarding running with or without collars. The following are the current collar requirements:

AKC
Flat buckle collar without tags or rivets or may run without collar. No tabs, leashes, or attachments of any kind allowed.

NADAC
No collars allowed.

UKC
Buckle collar required. No attachments. Tags strongly discouraged.

USDAA
No collars allowed.

AKC Classes

Class	Who may enter	Prerequisites
Novice A (standard)	Any dog without a title and handler who has never put a title on a dog	none
Novice B (standard)	Any dog without a title and a handler who has put an agility title on a dog in AKC	none
Open (standard)	Dog with an NA	Novice Agility title
Excellent A (standard)	Dog with OA. Cannot have AX.	Open Agility title
Excellent B (standard)	Dog with AX, MX, or MACH	Agility Excellent title
Novice A (jumpers)	Any dog without a title and handler who has never put a title on a dog	none
Novice B (jumpers)	Any dog without a title and a handler who has put an agility title on a dog in AKC	none
Open (jumpers)	Dog with an NAJ	Novice Agility Jumpers title
Excellent A (jumpers)	Dog with OAJ. Cannot have AXJ.	Open Agility Jumpers title
Excellent B (jumpers)	Dog with AXJ, MXJ, or MACH	Agility Excellent Jumpers title

AKC Height at Withers	Jump Height
10 inches and under	8 inches
14 inches and under	12 inches
18 inches and under	16 inches
20 inches and under	22 inches
Over 22 inches	24 inches

A dog may earn standard and jumpers titles simultaneously. Thus, a novice dog may compete in both Novice Standard and Novice Jumpers with Weaves at the same trial. None of the titles, except the MACH title, limit the dog's ability to earn further titles. (A dog must first have both his AX and AXJ in order to compete for a MACH.) So, if Ace is able to earn his Novice Standard first, he can still go into Open Standard while also competing for his Novice Jumpers with Weaves title.

The Judging Standards

Novice Standard

- Total score is 100 points
- Minimum qualifying score is 85 points
- 13–15 obstacles, no weave poles, no triple bar jump
- Novice dogs are allowed contact familiarization
- Timing: 2 yards per second plus 5 seconds
- Traps: No traps are allowed

The AKC Agility Nationals.

- Call-offs: Minor call-offs are allowed
- Point deductions include:
  - 1 point is deducted for each second overtime
  - 5 points are deducted for each run-out/refusal
  - 5 points are deducted for each off-course
  - 2 point deduction for each table fault (anticipating the count, jumping off table while counting)
- Elimination includes:
  - Knocked down bars
  - Walked over broad jump
  - Missed contacts (exception: upside of A-frame)
  - Excessive handling
  - Exceeding 2 run-outs/refusals
  - Exceeding 3 off-courses
  - Fly-offs
  - Handler touching the dog/obstacle

- Excusals include:
  - Dog leaving the course area
  - Out-of-control dog
  - Exceeding maximum course time

TIP: The Four-Paw Rule in AKC and USDAA

The "four-paw rule" is found in AKC and USDAA where if the dog puts all four paws on a contact obstacle and then bails off, the handler may not put the dog back on the contact obstacle. Instead, the judge will ask the handler to continue the course, although the dog is eliminated in AKC (in UKC, the Starters/Novice dog receives 20 faults). If the handler directs the dog back to the contact obstacle, the judge will excuse the handler.

– Fouling the ring (urinating, defecating, or vomiting)
– Failure to abide by the four paw rule

Novice Jumpers
• Total score is 100 points
• Minimum qualifying score is 85 points
• 13–15 obstacles, 6 weave poles, no triple bar jump, single bar jumps permitted
• A dog can have as many refusals on the weave poles and not have them count as refusals other than the time penalty.
• Timing is as follows:

Height Division	Speed in yards per second
8 inch	2.5
12 inch	2.5
16 inch	2.75
20 inch	3.0
24 inch	3.0

• Point deductions include:
– 1 point is deducted for each second overtime
– 5 points are deducted for each run-out/refusal
• Elimination includes:
– Knocked down bars
– Walked over broad jump
– Off-courses
– Excessive handling
– Exceeding 2 run-outs/refusals
– Handler touching the dog/obstacle
• Excusals include:
– Dog leaving the course area
– Out-of-control dog
– Exceeding maximum course time
– Fouling the ring (urinating, defecating, or vomiting)

Open Standard
• Total score is 100 points
• Minimum qualifying score is 85 points
• 16–18 obstacles, includes weave poles and triple bar jump
• Timing is as follows:

Height Division	Speed in yards per second
8 inch	2.25 plus 5 seconds for pause table
12 inch	2.25 plus 5 seconds for pause table
16 inch	2.35 plus 5 seconds for pause table
20 inch	2.5 plus 5 seconds for pause table
24 inch	2.5 plus 5 seconds for pause table

• Point deductions include:
– 2 points are deducted for each second overtime
– 5 points are deducted for each run-out/refusal
– 5 points are deducted for each off-course
– 2 point deduction for each table fault (anticipating the count, jumping off table while counting)
• Elimination includes:
– Knocked down bars
– Walked over broad jump
– Missed contacts (exception: upside of A-frame)
– Excessive handling
– Exceeding 1 run-out/refusal
– Exceeding 2 off-courses
– Fly-offs
– Handler touching the dog/obstacle

AKC Titles

Your dog can earn the following titles in AKC Agility:

Title	Abbreviation	Requirements
Novice Agility	NA	Completion of three novice legs with qualifying score
Open Agility	OA	Completion of three open legs with qualifying score and an NA
Agility Excellent	AX	Completion of three excellent legs with qualifying score and an OA
Master's Agility Excellent	MX	10 qualifying scores in the excellent class and an AX
Novice Agility Jumpers with Weaves	NAJ	Completion of three novice jumpers legs with qualifying score
Open Agility Jumpers with Weaves	OAJ	Completion of three open jumpers legs with qualifying score and an NAJ
Agility Dog Excellent Jumpers with Weaves	AXJ	Completion of three excellent jumpers legs with qualifying score and an OAJ
Masters Agility Excellent Jumpers with Weaves	MXJ	10 qualifying scores in the excellent class and an AXJ
Master's Agility Champion	MACH	20 double qualifying runs (a qualifying excellent B and excellent B jumpers with weaves in the same day) and 750 points

• Excusals include:
  – Dog leaving the course area
  – Out-of-control dog
  – Exceeding maximum course time
  – Fouling the ring (urinating, defecating, or vomiting)
  – Failure to abide by the four paw rule

Open Jumpers
• Total score is 100 points
• Minimum qualifying score is 85 points
• 16–18 obstacles, 6–12 weave poles, triple bar jump, single bar jumps and one bar jump permitted

• Timing is as follows:

Height Division	Speed in yards per second
8 inch	3.0
12 inch	3.0
16 inch	3.25
20 inch	3.5
24 inch	3.5

• Point deductions include:
  – 2 points are deducted for each second overtime

– 5 points are deducted for each run-out/refusal
- Elimination includes:
  – Knocked down bars
  – Walked over broad jump
  – Off-courses
  – Excessive handling
  – Exceeding 1 run-out/refusal
  – Handler touching the dog/obstacle
- Excusals include:
  – Dog leaving the course area
  – Out-of-control dog
  – Exceeding maximum course time
  – Fouling the ring (urinating, defecating, or vomiting)

Excellent Standard
- Total score is 100 points
- Minimum qualifying score is 85 points
- 18–20 obstacles, includes weave poles, one bar jump, and triple bar jump
- Timing is as follows:

Height Division	Speed in yards per second
8 inch	2.50 plus 5 seconds for pause table
12 inch	2.50 plus 5 seconds for pause table
16 inch	2.75 plus 5 seconds for pause table
20 inch	3.0 plus 5 seconds for pause table
24 inch	3.0 plus 5 seconds for pause table

- Point deductions include:
  – 3 points are deducted for each second overtime
  – 5 points are deducted for each run-out/refusal

– 5 points are deducted for each off-course
– 2 point deduction for each table fault (anticipating the count, jumping off table while counting)
- Elimination includes:
  – Knocked down bars
  – Walked over broad jump
  – Missed contacts (exception: upside of A-frame)
  – Excessive handling
  – Any run-out/refusals
  – Exceeding 1 off-course
  – Fly-offs
  – Handler touching the dog/obstacle
- Excusals include:
  – Dog leaving the course area
  – Out-of-control dog
  – Exceeding maximum course time
  – Fouling the ring (urinating, defecating, or vomiting)
  – Failure to abide by the four paw rule

Excellent Jumpers
- Total score is 100 points
- Minimum qualifying score is 100 points
- 18–20 obstacles, 9–12 weave poles, triple bar jump, single bar jumps, and one bar jump permitted
- Timing is as follows:

Height Division	Speed in yards per second
8 inch	3.25
12 inch	3.25
16 inch	3.50
20 inch	3.75
24 inch	3.75

- Point deductions include:
  – 3 points are deducted for each second overtime

- 5 points are deducted for each run-out/refusal
- Elimination includes:
  - Knocked down bars
  - Walked over broad jump
  - Off-courses
  - Excessive handling
  - Any run-outs/refusals
  - Handler touching the dog/obstacle
- Excusals include:
  - Dog leaving the course area
  - Out-of-control dog
  - Exceeding maximum course time
  - Fouling the ring (urinating, defecating, or vomiting)

NADAC

The Classes

NADAC has divided their standards into levels, divisions, and classes. The classes are Regular Agility, Gamblers, and Jumpers. Within those classes are Novice, Open, and Elite (Elite being similar to Excellent in AKC and USDAA). NADAC further differentiates these with divisions: Standard, Veterans, and Junior Handlers.

NADAC has the most titles in any organization, as dogs below the Elite level may obtain certifications in the nonstandard classes. Within the levels, there is further differentiation of performance. A dog may have a Novice Agility Certificate or one with Outstanding or Superior Performance. So, a dog could obtain many titles at various levels and degrees of performance. Once a dog obtains a title at a certain level (e.g. Novice) the handler can opt to continue to

> ### TIP: Judge's Hand Signals
>
> The judge will show faults as they occur. The following are the standard hand signals:
> - Fist in the air: refusal or run-out
> - Open hand in the air: off-course (AKC)
> - Two open hands in the air: NQ
> - Judge puts hands together in a T: table fault
> - Open hand in air: 5 points off (NADAC and USDAA)
>
> Consult each organization's rulebook for the meaning of individual hand signals. For example, in UKC, a judge will verbally call a fault, whereas in other organizations a judge will use hand signals.

work towards Novice Agility Certificate Outstanding Performance or move into the Open level class. The dog becomes ineligible to receive any further Novice points once it obtains points in Open level class.

The A/B class division is at the sole discretion of the hosting group. Conceivably, all levels could be divided out into A and B, only Novice levels divided into A and B, or no levels divided. The A/B division allows a fair placement for ribbons. Anyone within the competition level may compete in the B class; A is reserved for handlers who have not put a title on their dogs.

A dog can only be entered in one division and in one height. Veteran's class is defined as dogs over 7 years of age or handlers over 60 years of age. Junior Handler class is for anyone 17 years of age or younger.

NADAC Classes

Class	Who may enter	Prerequisites
Standard Division		
Novice A	Any dog without a title and handler who has never put a title on a dog	None
Novice B	Any dog without a title and a handler who has put an agility title on a dog. Dog with an O-NAC or better.	None
Open A	Dog with an NAC	Novice Agility Certificate
Open B	Dog with an OAC or O-OAC or handler who has put an agility title on a dog	Open Agility Certificate
Elite A	Dog with an OAC	Open Agility Certificate
Elite B	Dog with an EAC or S-EAC or handler who has put an agility title on a dog	Elite Agility Certificate
Novice Gamblers A	Any dog without a title and handler who has never put a title on a dog	None
Novice Gamblers B	Any dog without a title and a handler who has put an agility title on a dog. Dog with an O-NGC or greater.	None
Open Gamblers A	Dog with an NGC	Novice Gamblers Certificate
Open Gamblers B	Dog with an OGC or O-OGC or handler who has put an agility title on a dog	Open Gamblers Certificate
Elite Gamblers A	Dog with an OGC	Open Gamblers Certificate
Elite Gamblers B	Dog with an EAC or S-EAC or handler who has put an agility title on a dog	Elite Gamblers Certificate
Novice Jumpers A	Any dog without a title and handler who has never put a title on a dog	None
Novice Jumpers B	Any dog without a title and a handler who has put an agility title on a dog. Dog with an O-NJC or greater.	None
Open Jumpers A	Dog with an NJC	Novice Jumpers Certificate
Open Jumpers B	Dog with an OJC or O-OJC or handler who has put an agility title on a dog	Open Jumpers Certificate
Elite Jumpers A	Dog with an OJC	Open Jumpers Certificate
Elite Jumpers B	Dog with an EJC or S-EJC or handler who has put an agility title on a dog	Elite Jumpers Certificate

NADAC Classes (continued)

Class	Who may enter	Prerequisites
Veterans Division		
Veterans Novice A	Any dog without a title and handler who has never put a title on a dog	None
Veterans Novice B	Any dog without a title and a handler who has put an agility title on a dog. Dog with an O-NAC-V or better.	None
Veterans Open A	Dog with an NAC-V	Veterans Novice Agility Certificate
Veterans Open B	Dog with an OAC-V or O-OAC-V or handler who has put an agility title on a dog	Veterans Open Agility Certificate
Veterans Elite A	Dog with an S-OAC-V or handler who has put an agility title on a dog	Veterans Open Agility Certificate
Veterans Elite B	Dog with an EAC-V or S-EAC-V or handler who has put an agility title on a dog	Veterans Elite Agility Certificate
Veterans Novice Gamblers A	Any dog without a title and handler who has never put a title on a dog	None
Veterans Novice Gamblers B	Any dog without a title and a handler who has put an agility title on a dog. Dog with an O-NGC-V or greater.	None
Veterans Open Gamblers A	Dog with an NGC-V	Veterans Novice Gamblers Certificate
Veterans Open Gamblers B	Dog with an OGC-V or O-OGC-V or handler who has put an agility title on a dog	Veterans Open Gamblers Certificate
Veterans Elite Gamblers A	Dog with an OGC-V	Veterans Open Gamblers Certificate
Veterans Elite Gamblers B	Dog with an EAC-V or S-EAC-V or handler who has put an agility title on a dog	Veterans Elite Gamblers Certificate
Veterans Novice Jumpers A	Any dog without a title and handler who has never put a title on a dog	None
Veterans Novice Jumpers B	Any dog without a title and a handler who has put an agility title on a dog. Dog with an O-NJC-V or greater.	None

NADAC Classes (continued)

Class	Who may enter	Prerequisites
Veterans Open Jumpers A	Dog with an NJC-V	Veterans Novice Jumpers Certificate
Veterans Open Jumpers B	Dog with an OJC-V or O-OJC-v or handler who has put an agility title on a dog	Veterans Open Jumpers Certificate
Veterans Elite Jumpers A	Dog with an OJC-V	Veterans Open Jumpers Certificate
Veterans Elite Jumpers B	Dog with an EJC-V or S-EJC-V or handler who has put an agility title on a dog	Veterans Elite Jumpers Certificate

Junior Handler Division

Class	Who may enter	Prerequisites
Junior Handler Novice A	Any dog without a title and handler who has never put a title on a dog	None
Junior Handler Novice B	Any dog without a title and a handler who has put an agility title on a dog. Dog with an O-NAC-JH or better.	None
Junior Handler Open A	Dog with an NAC-JH	Junior Handler Novice Agility Certificate
Junior Handler Open B	Dog with an OAC-JH or O-OAC-JH or handler who has put an agility title on a dog	Junior Handler Open Agility Certificate
Junior Handler Elite A	Dog with an OAC-JH	Junior Handler Open Agility Certificate
Junior Handler Elite B	Dog with an EAC-JH or S-EAC-JH or handler who has put an agility title on a dog	Junior Handler Elite Agility Certificate
Junior Handler Novice Jumpers A	Any dog without a title and handler who has never put a title on a dog	None
Junior Handler Novice Jumpers B	Any dog without a title and a handler who has put an agility title on a dog. Dog with an O-NJC-JH or greater.	None
Junior Handler Open Jumpers A	Dog with an NJC-JH	Junior Handler Novice Jumpers Certificate
Junior Handler Open Jumpers B	Dog with an OJC-JH or O-OJC-JH or handler who has put an agility title on a dog	Junior Handler Open Jumpers Certificate

NADAC Classes (continued)

Class	Who may enter	Prerequisites
Junior Handler Elite Jumpers A	Dog with an OJC-JH	Junior Handler Open Jumpers Certificate
Junior Handler Elite Jumpers B	Dog with an EJC-JH or S-EJC-JH or handler who has put an agility title on a dog	Junior Handler Elite Jumpers Certificate

NADAC Standard Height at Withers	Jump Height
11 inches and under	8 inches
13 inches and under	12 inches
17 inches and under	16 inches
20 inches and under	22 inches
Over 20 inches	24 inches

NADAC Veterans and Junior Handler's Height at Withers	Jump Height
11 inches and under	4 inches
13 inches and under	8 inches
17 inches and under	12 inches
20 inches and under	16 inches
Over 20 inches	20 inches

Jump Height Exemption List: NADAC gives a special exemption to certain dog breeds, allowing them to jump at 4 inches less than the current heights. This exemption includes the following breeds and those dogs that weigh three times or more the amount of their height in inches:

- Akita
- Alaskan Malamute
- Basset Hound
- Bernese Mountain Dog
- Bloodhound
- Bulldog
- Bullmastiff
- Bull Terrier
- Cardigan Welsh Corgi
- Clumber Spaniel
- Free Bulldog
- Great Dane
- Greater Swiss Mountain Dog
- Great Pyrenees
- Irish Wolfhound
- Kuvasz
- Leonberger
- Mastiff
- Newfoundland
- Otter Hounds
- Rottweiler
- Saint Bernard
- Bouvier
- Pug
- German Shepherd Dog
- Petite Basset Griffon Vendeen
- Pembroke Welsh Corgi

NADAC Titles

Title	Abbreviation	Requirements
Standard/Regular Agility		
Novice Agility Certificate	NAC	30 combined points earned in Novice classes under at least 2 different judges
Novice Agility Certificate Outstanding Performance	O-NAC	100 combined points earned in Novice classes under at least 2 different judges
Novice Agility Certificate Superior Performance	S-NAC	200 combined points earned in Novice classes under at least 2 different judges
Open Agility Certificate	OAC	30 combined points earned in Open classes under at least 2 different judges
Open Agility Certificate Outstanding Performance	O-OAC	100 combined points earned in Open classes under at least 2 different judges
Open Agility Certificate Superior Performance	S-OAC	200 combined points earned in Open classes under at least 2 different judges
Elite Agility Certificate	EAC	30 combined points earned in Elite classes under at least 2 different judges
Elite Agility Certificate Outstanding Performance	O-EAC	100 combined points earned in Elite classes underat least 2 different judges
Elite Agility Certificate Superior Performance	S-EAC	200 combined points earned in Elite classes underat least 2 different judges
Veterans/Regular Agility		
Veterans Novice Agility Certificate	NAC-V	30 combined points earned in Veterans Novice classes under at least 2 different judges
Veterans Novice Agility Certificate Outstanding Performance	O-NAC-V	100 combined points earned in Veterans Novice classes under at least 2 different judges
Veterans Novice Agility Certificate Superior Performance	S-NAC-V	200 combined points earned in Veterans Novice classes under at least 2 different judges
Veterans Open Agility Certificate	OAC-V	30 combined points earned in Veterans Open classes under at least 2 different judges
Veterans Open Agility Certificate Outstanding Performance	O-OAC-V	100 combined points earned in Veterans Open classes under at least 2 different judges

NADAC Titles (continued)

Title	Abbreviation	Requirements
Veterans Open Agility Certificate Superior Performance	S-OAC-V	200 combined points earned in Veterans Open classes under at least 2 different judges
Veterans Elite Agility Certificate	EAC-V	30 combined points earned in Veterans Elite classes under at least 2 different judges
Veterans Elite Agility Certificate Outstanding Performance	O-EAC-V	100 combined points earned in Veterans Elite classes under at least 2 different judges
Veterans Elite Agility Certificate Superior Performance	S-EAC-V	200 combined points earned in Veterans Elite classes under at least 2 different judges

Junior Handlers/Regular Agility

Title	Abbreviation	Requirements
Junior Handler's Novice Agility Certificate	NAC-JH	30 combined points earned in Junior Handlers Novice classes under at least 2 different judges
Junior Handler's Agility Certificate Outstanding Performance	O-NAC-JH	100 combined points earned in Junior Handlers Novice classes under at least 2 different judges
Junior Handler's Novice Agility Certificate Superior Performance	S-NAC-JH	200 combined points earned in Junior Handlers Novice classes under at least 2 different judges
Junior Handler's Open Agility Certificate	OAC-JH	30 combined points earned in Junior Handlers Open classes under at least 2 different judges
Junior Handler's Open Agility Certificate Outstanding Performance	O-OAC-JH	100 combined points earned in Junior Handlers Open classes under at least 2 different judges
Junior Handler's Open Agility Certificate Superior Performance	S-OAC-JH	200 combined points earned in Junior Handlers Open classes under at least 2 different judges
Junior Handler's Elite Agility Certificate	EAC-JH	30 combined points earned in Junior Handlers Elite classes under at least 2 different judges
Junior Handler's Elite Agility Certificate Outstanding Performance	O-EAC-JH	100 combined points earned in Junior Handlers Elite classes under at least 2 different judges

NADAC Titles (continued)

Title	Abbreviation	Requirements
Junior Handler's Elite Agility Certificate Superior Performance	S-EAC-JH	200 combined points earned in Junior Handlers Elite classes under at least 2 different judges
Standard/Jumpers		
Novice Jumpers Certificate	NJC	20 combined points earned in Novice Jumpers classes
Novice Jumpers Certificate Outstanding Performance	O-NJC	50 combined points earned in Novice Jumpers classes
Novice Jumpers Certificate Superior Performance	S-NJC	100 combined points earned in Novice Jumpers classes
Open Jumpers Certificate	OJC	20 combined points earned in Open Jumpers classes
Open Jumpers Certificate Outstanding Performance	O-OJC	50 combined points earned in Open Jumpers classes
Open Jumpers Certificate Superior Performance	S-OJC	100 combined points earned in Open Jumpers classes
Elite Jumpers Certificate	EJC	20 combined points earned in Elite Jumpers classes
Elite Jumpers Certificate	O-EJC	50 combined points earned in Elite Jumpers classes
Elite Jumpers Certificate	S-EJC	100 combined points earned in Elite Jumpers classes
Veterans/Jumpers		
Veterans Novice Jumpers Certificate	NJC-V	20 combined points earned in Veterans Novice Jumpers classes
Veterans Novice Jumpers Certificate Outstanding Performance	O-NJC-V	50 combined points earned in Veterans Novice Jumpers classes
Veterans Novice Jumpers Certificate Superior Performance	S-NJC-V	100 combined points earned in Veterans Novice Jumpers classes
Veterans Open Jumpers Certificate	OJC-V	20 combined points earned in Veterans Open Jumpers classes
Veterans Open Jumpers Certificate Outstanding Performance	O-OJC-V	50 combined points earned in Veterans Open Jumpers classes under at least 2 different judges

NADAC Titles (continued)

Title	Abbreviation	Requirements
Veterans Open Jumpers Certificate Superior Performance	S-OJC-V	100 combined points earned in Veterans Open Jumpers classes
Veterans Elite Jumpers Certificate	EJC-V	20 combined points earned in Veterans Elite Jumpers classes
Veterans Elite Jumpers Certificate	O-EJC-V	50 combined points earned in Veterans Elite Jumpers classes
Veterans Elite Jumpers Certificate	S-EJC-V	100 combined points earned in Veterans Elite Jumpers classes

Junior Handler/Jumpers

Title	Abbreviation	Requirements
Junior Handler Novice Jumpers Certificate	NJC-JH	20 combined points earned in Junior Handlers Novice Jumpers classes
Junior Handler Novice Jumpers Certificate Outstanding Performance	O-NJC-JH	50 combined points earned in Junior Handlers Novice Jumpers classes
Junior Handler Novice Jumpers Certificate Superior Performance	S-NJC-JH	100 combined points earned in Junior Handlers Novice Jumpers classes
Junior Handler Open Jumpers Certificate	OJC-JH	20 combined points earned in Junior Handlers Open Jumpers classes
Junior Handler Open Jumpers Certificate Outstanding Performance	O-OJC-JH	50 combined points earned in Junior Handlers Open Jumpers classes
Junior Handler Open Jumpers Certificate Superior Performance	S-OJC-JH	100 combined points earned in Junior Handlers Open Jumpers classes
Junior Handler Elite Jumpers Certificate	EJC-JH	20 combined points earned in Junior Handlers Elite Jumpers classes
Junior Handler Elite Jumpers Certificate	O-EJC-JH	50 combined points earned in Junior Handlers Elite Jumpers classes
Junior Handler Elite Jumpers Certificate	S-EJC-JH	100 combined points earned in Junior Handlers Elite Jumpers classes

Standard/Gamblers

Title	Abbreviation	Requirements
Novice Gamblers Certificate	NGC	20 combined points earned in Novice Gamblers classes

NADAC Titles (continued)

Title	Abbreviation	Requirements
Novice Gamblers Certificate Outstanding Performance	O-NGC	50 combined points earned in Novice Gamblers classes
Novice Gamblers Certificate Superior Performance	S-NGC	100 combined points earned in Novice Gamblers classes
Open Gamblers Certificate	OGC	20 combined points earned in Open Gamblers classes
Open Gamblers Certificate Outstanding Performance	O-OGC	50 combined points earned in Open Gamblers classes
Open Gamblers Certificate Superior Performance	S-OGC	100 combined points earned in Open Gamblers classes
Elite Gamblers Certificate	EGC	20 combined points earned in Elite Gamblers classes
Elite Gamblers Certificate	O-EGC	50 combined points earned in Elite Gamblers classes
Elite Gamblers Certificate	S-EGC	100 combined points earned in Elite Gamblers classes

Veterans/Gamblers

Title	Abbreviation	Requirements
Veterans Novice Gamblers Certificate	NGC-V	20 combined points earned in Veterans Novice Gamblers classes
Veterans Novice Gamblers Certificate Outstanding Performance	O-NGC-V	50 combined points earned in Veterans Novice Gamblers classes
Veterans Novice Gamblers Certificate Superior Performance	S-NGC-V	100 combined points earned in Veterans Novice Gamblers classes
Veterans Open Gamblers Certificate	OGC-V	20 combined points earned in Veterans Open Gamblers classes
Veterans Open Gamblers Certificate Outstanding Performance	O-OGC-V	50 combined points earned in Veterans Open Gamblers classes
Veterans Open Gamblers Certificate Superior Performance	S-OGC-V	100 combined points earned in Veterans Open Gamblers classes
Veterans Elite Gamblers Certificate	EGC-V	20 combined points earned in Veterans Elite Gamblers classes

NADAC Titles (continued)

Title	Abbreviation	Requirements
Veterans Elite Gamblers Certificate	O-EGC-V	50 combined points earned in Veterans Elite Gamblers classes
Veterans Elite Gamblers Certificate	S-EGC-V	100 combined points earned in Veterans Elite Gamblers classes

Championship Titles
Standard Division

Title	Abbreviation	Requirements
Agility Trial Champion	NATCH	Cumulative points must be earned in the following Elite Classes: • 230 points in Regular Agility • 120 points in Jumpers • 120 points in Gamblers
Agility Trial Champion—Outstanding Performance	O-NATCH	Cumulative points must be earned in the following Elite Classes: • 430 points in Regular Agility • 230 points in Jumpers • 230 points in Gamblers
Agility Trial Champion—Superior Performance	S-NATCH	Cumulative points must be earned in the following Elite Classes: • 630 points in Regular Agility • 320 points in Jumpers • 320 points in Gamblers

Veterans Division

Title	Abbreviation	Requirements
Veteran Agility Trial Champion	V-NATCH	Cumulative points must be earned in the following Veteran Elite Classes: • 230 points in Regular Agility • 120 points in Jumpers • 120 points in Gamblers
Veteran Agility Trial Champion—Outstanding Performance	O-V-NATCH	Cumulative points must be earned in the following Veteran Elite Classes: • 430 points in Regular Agility • 230 points in Jumpers • 230 points in Gamblers
Veteran Agility Trial Champion—Superior Performance	S-V-NATCH	Cumulative points must be earned in the following Veteran Elite Classes: • 630 points in Regular Agility • 320 points in Jumpers • 320 points in Gamblers

NADAC Titles (continued)

Title	Abbreviation	Requirements
Junior Handlers Division		
Junior Handlers Agility Trial Champion	JH-NATCH	Cumulative points must be earned in the following Junior Handlers Elite Classes: • 230 points in Regular Agility • 120 points in Jumpers • 120 points in Gamblers
Junior Handlers Agility Trial Champion—Outstanding Performance	O-JH-NATCH	Cumulative points must be earned in the following Junior Handlers Elite Classes: • 430 points in Regular Agility • 230 points in Jumpers • 230 points in Gamblers
Junior Handlers Agility Trial Champion—Superior Performance	S-JH-NATCH	Cumulative points must be earned in the following Junior Handlers Elite Classes: • 630 points in Regular Agility • 320 points in Jumpers • 320 points in Gamblers
1000 Point Certificate		Dog that has earned 1000 cumulative points
2000 Point Certificate		Dog that has earned 2000 cumulative points

The Judging Standards

Novice Level Regular Agility Class (Standard, Veterans, and Junior Handler)
- Total score is 10 points
- Dogs earning 5 or less faults receive 5 points
- 12–13 obstacles
- Timing: 2.25–2.75 yards per second. Dogs in the 16-inch jump heights and below are allowed 5 extra seconds on courses under 160 feet and 8 seconds on courses over 160 feet. Veterans and Junior Handlers times are 10 percent more.
- Traps: allowed, but require adequate spacing
- Call-offs: minor call-offs are allowed
- Point deductions include:
  - 1 fault or fraction of a fault is deducted for each second (or fraction thereof) overtime
  - 10 faults are deducted for missed safety zone (downside of the contacts for contact obstacles). 10 faults are also assessed for incidental contact of the safety zone.
  - 10 faults are deducted for each off-course
  - 5 faults for one or more missed weave poles
  - 5 faults for accidentally touching the dog
  - 5 faults for physically assisting the dog at the starting line
  - 5 faults for assistance from spectators
  - 5 faults for dog nipping the handler
  - 5 faults for out-of-control dog as demonstrated by repeated recalls or downs
  - 5 faults for blocking the dog
  - 20 faults for foul language, display of anger, or harsh commands
  - 20 faults for unsafe performance of the obstacle
  - 5 faults for knocked down bar
  - 20 faults for fly-offs or failure to complete an obstacle
- Excusals include:
  - Poor sportsmanship
  - Aggression
  - Dog leaving the course area
  - Out-of-control dog
  - Exceeding maximum course time
  - Fouling the ring (urinating, defecating, or vomiting)
  - Excessive training in the ring
  - Retrying contact obstacle after a failure to complete

Novice Level Jumpers Class (Standard, Veterans, and Junior Handler)
- Total score is 10 points
- Dogs earning 5 or less faults receive 5 points
- 12–13 obstacles
- Timing: 3.50–4.0 yards per second. Dogs in the 16-inch jump heights and below are allowed 5 extra seconds on courses under 160 feet and 8 seconds on courses over 160 feet. Veterans and Junior Handlers times are 10 percent more.
- Traps: allowed
- Call-offs: call-offs are allowed
- Point deductions include:
  - 1 fault or fraction of a fault is deducted for each second (or fraction thereof) overtime
  - 10 faults are deducted for missed safety zone (downside of the contacts for contact obstacles). 10 faults are also assessed for incidental contact of the safety zone.
  - 10 faults are deducted for each off-course

- 5 faults for one or more missed weave poles
- 5 faults for accidentally touching the dog
- 5 faults for physically assisting the dog at the starting line
- 5 faults for assistance from spectators
- 5 faults for dog nipping the handler
- 5 faults for out-of-control dog as demonstrated by repeated recalls or downs
- 5 faults for blocking the dog
- 20 faults for foul language, display of anger, or harsh commands
- 20 faults for unsafe performance of the obstacle
- 5 faults for knocked down bar
- 20 faults for fly-offs or failure to complete an obstacle
- Excusals include:
  - Poor sportsmanship
  - Aggression
  - Dog leaving the course area
  - Out-of-control dog
  - Exceeding maximum course time
  - Fouling the ring (urinating, defecating, or vomiting)
  - Excessive training in the ring
  - Retrying contact obstacle after a failure to complete

Novice Level Gamblers Class (Standard and Veterans)
- Total qualifying points earned is 10 points
- In order to qualify, the dog must earn 20 opening points and 20 gamble points
- No weaves, teeter, or tire allowed
- Gamble distance: 10 feet
- Timing: 40 seconds during point accumulation period. Dogs in the 16-inch jump heights and below are allowed 45 sec-

onds. Veterans times are 2 seconds more to perform the gamble.
- Point accumulations include:
  - Jumps: 1 point
  - Tunnel, chute, tire, short weave poles: 3 points
  - Dog walk, A-frame, teeter, long weave poles: 5 points
  - Gamble points include:
  - First Obstacle: 2 points
  - Second Obstacle: 4 points
  - Third Obstacle: 6 points
  - Fourth Obstacle: 8 points
  - Bonus Obstacle (if available): 10 points
- Excusals include:
  - Poor sportsmanship
  - Aggression
  - Dog leaving the course area
  - Out-of-control dog
  - Exceeding maximum course time
  - Fouling the ring (urinating, defecating, or vomiting)
  - Excessive training in the ring

Open Level Regular Agility Class (Standard, Veterans, and Junior Handler)
- Total score is 10 points
- Dogs earning 5 or less faults receive 5 points
- 13–14 obstacles
- Timing: 2.75–3.25 yards per second. Dogs in the 16-inch jump heights and below are allowed 5 extra seconds on courses under 160 feet and 8 seconds on courses over 160 feet. Veterans and Junior Handlers times are 10 percent more.
- Traps: Minor traps are allowed
- Call-offs: call-offs are allowed
- Point deductions include:
  - 1 fault or fraction of a fault is deducted for each second (or fraction thereof) over time

- 10 faults are deducted for missed safety zone (downside of the contacts for contact obstacles). 10 faults are also assessed for incidental contact of the safety zone.
- 10 faults are deducted for each off-course
- 5 faults for one or more missed weave poles
- 5 faults for accidentally touching the dog
- 5 faults for physically assisting the dog at the starting line
- 5 faults for assistance from spectators
- 5 faults for dog nipping the handler
- 5 faults for out-of-control dog as demonstrated by repeated recalls or downs
- 5 faults for blocking the dog
- 20 faults for foul language, display of anger, or harsh commands
- 20 faults for unsafe performance of the obstacle
- 5 faults for knocked down bar
- 20 faults for fly-offs or failure to complete an obstacle
- Excusals include:
  - Poor sportsmanship
  - Aggression
  - Dog leaving the course area
  - Out-of-control dog
  - Exceeding maximum course time
  - Fouling the ring (urinating, defecating, or vomiting)
  - Excessive training in the ring

Open Level Jumpers Class (Standard, Veterans, and Junior Handler)
- Total score is 10 points
- Dogs earning 5 or less faults receive 5 points

- 13–14 obstacles
- Timing: 4.0–4.5 yards per second. Dogs in the 16-inch jump heights and below are allowed 5 extra seconds on courses under 160 feet and 8 seconds on courses over 160 feet. Veterans and Junior Handlers times are 10 percent more.
- Traps: No traps are allowed
- Call-offs: minor call-offs are allowed
- Point deductions include:
  - 1 fault or fraction of a fault is deducted for each second (or fraction thereof) overtime
  - 10 faults are deducted for missed safety zone (downside of the contacts for contact obstacles). 10 faults are also assessed for incidental contact of the safety zone.
  - 10 faults are deducted for each off-course
  - 5 faults for one or more missed weave poles
  - 5 faults for accidentally touching the dog
  - 5 faults for physically assisting the dog at the starting line
  - 5 faults for assistance from spectators
  - 5 faults for dog nipping the handler
  - 5 faults for out-of-control dog as demonstrated by repeated recalls or downs
  - 5 faults for blocking the dog
  - 20 faults for foul language, display of anger, or harsh commands
  - 20 faults for unsafe performance of the obstacle
  - 5 faults for knocked down bar
  - 20 faults for failure to complete an obstacle
- Excusals include:
  - Poor sportsmanship

- Aggression
- Dog leaving the course area
- Out-of-control dog
- Exceeding maximum course time
- Fouling the ring (urinating, defecating, or vomiting)
- Excessive training in the ring

Open Level Gamblers Class
(Standard and Veterans)

- Total qualifying points earned is 10 points
- In order to qualify, the dog must earn 24 opening points and 20 gamble points
- No tire allowed; short line of weave poles (5–6) are permitted
- Gamble distance: 15 feet
- Timing: 40 seconds during point accumulation period. Dogs in the 16-inch jump heights and below are allowed 45 seconds. Veterans times are 2 seconds more to perform the gamble.
- Point accumulations include:
  - Jumps: 1 point
  - Tunnel, chute, 5–6 weave poles: 3 points
  - Dog walk, A-frame, teeter: 5 points
- Gamble points include:
  - First Obstacle: 2 points
  - Second Obstacle: 4 points
  - Third Obstacle: 6 points
  - Fourth Obstacle: 8 points
  - Bonus Obstacle (if available): 10 points
- Excusals include:
  - Poor sportsmanship
  - Aggression
  - Dog leaving the course area
  - Out-of-control dog
  - Exceeding maximum course time
  - Fouling the ring (urinating, defecating, or vomiting)
  - Excessive training in the ring

Elite Level Regular Agility Class
(Standard, Veterans, and Junior Handler)

- Total score is 10 points
- Dogs earning 5 or less faults receive 5 points
- 14–15 obstacles
- Timing: 3.25–3.75 yards per second. Dogs in the 16-inch jump heights and below are allowed 5 extra seconds on courses under 160 feet and 8 seconds on courses over 160 feet. Veterans and Junior Handlers times are 10 percent more.
- Traps: traps are allowed
- Call-offs: call-offs are allowed
- Point deductions include:
  - 1 fault or fraction of a fault is deducted for each second (or fraction thereof) overtime
  - 10 faults are deducted for missed safety zone (downside of the contacts for contact obstacles). 10 faults are also assessed for incidental contact of the safety zone.
  - 10 faults are deducted for each off-course
  - 5 faults for one or more missed weave poles
  - 5 faults for accidentally touching the dog
  - 5 faults for physically assisting the dog at the starting line
  - 5 faults for assistance from spectators
  - 5 faults for dog nipping the handler
  - 5 faults for out-of-control dog as demonstrated by repeated recalls or downs
  - 5 faults for blocking the dog
  - 20 faults for foul language, display of anger, or harsh commands
  - 20 faults for unsafe performance of the obstacle
  - 5 faults for knocked down bar

– 20 faults for fly-offs or failure to complete an obstacle
- Excusals include:
  – Poor sportsmanship
  – Aggression
  – Dog leaving the course area
  – Out-of-control dog
  – Exceeding maximum course time
  – Fouling the ring (urinating, defecating, or vomiting)
  – Excessive training in the ring

Elite Level Jumpers Class
(Standard, Veterans, and Junior Handler)
- Total score is 10 points
- Dogs earning 5 or less faults receive 5 points
- 14–15 obstacles
- Timing: 4.5–5.0 yards per second. Dogs in the 16-inch jump heights and below are allowed 5 extra seconds on courses under 160 feet and 8 seconds on courses over 160 feet. Veterans and Junior Handlers times are 10 percent more.
- Traps: No traps are allowed
- Call-offs: minor call-offs are allowed
- Point deductions include:
  – 1 fault or fraction of a fault is deducted for each second (or fraction thereof) overtime
  – 10 faults are deducted for missed safety zone (downside of the contacts for contact obstacles). 10 faults are also assessed for incidental contact of the safety zone.
  – 10 faults are deducted for each off-course
  – 5 faults for one or more missed weave poles
  – 5 faults for accidentally touching the dog

– 5 faults for physically assisting the dog at the starting line
– 5 faults for assistance from spectators
– 5 faults for dog nipping the handler
– 5 faults for out-of-control dog as demonstrated by repeated recalls or downs
– 5 faults for blocking the dog
– 20 faults for foul language, display of anger, or harsh commands
– 20 faults for unsafe performance of the obstacle
– 5 faults for knocked down bar
– 20 faults for failure to complete an obstacle
- Excusals include:
  – Poor sportsmanship
  – Aggression
  – Dog leaving the course area
  – Out-of-control dog
  – Exceeding maximum course time
  – Fouling the ring (urinating, defecating, or vomiting)
  – Excessive training in the ring

Elite Level Gamblers Class
(Standard and Veterans)
- Total qualifying points earned is 10 points
- In order to qualify, the dog must earn 28 opening points and 20 gamble points
- All obstacles allowed
- Gamble distance: 20 feet
- Timing: 40 seconds during point accumulation period. Dogs in the 16-inch jump heights and below are allowed 45 seconds. Veterans times are 2 seconds more to perform the gamble.
- Point accumulations include:
  – Jumps: 1 point
  – Tunnel, chute, 5–6 weave poles, tire: 3 points

An agility trial walkthrough.

- Dog walk, A-frame, teeter, 10–12 weave poles: 5 points
- Gamble points include:
  - First Obstacle: 2 points
  - Second Obstacle: 4 points
  - Third Obstacle: 6 points
  - Fourth Obstacle: 8 points
  - Bonus Obstacle (if available): 10 points
- Excusals include:
  - Poor sportsmanship
  - Aggression
  - Dog leaving the course area
  - Out-of-control dog
  - Exceeding maximum course time
  - Fouling the ring (urinating, defecating, or vomiting)
  - Excessive training in the ring

UKC

The Classes

UKC has three classes: Agility I, Agility II, and Agility III. Agility I class has all contact obstacles, the pause table, hoop, closed and pipe tunnels, and most hurdles. Unlike other forms of agility, Agility I courses do not have tire obstacles. The Agility II class has the sway bridge, pause box, crawl tunnel, weave poles, platform jump, tire jump, swing plank, and all possible hurdles.

Agility III class has all the obstacles in both the Agility I and Agility II classes.

Unlike other styles of agility, UKC makes no differentiation between the beginner and the seasoned trainer with A and B classes.

A dog may work towards U-AGI and U-AGII titles simultaneously. However, a dog may not earn its U-AGII title before completing its U-AGI title. If a dog obtains its three legs for U-AGII, it must first obtain its legs in the U-AGI title before receiving its U-AGII certificate.

The Judging Standards

Agility I
- Total score is 200 points
- Minimum qualifying score is 170 points
- 13 obstacles as defined by AGI rules
- Dogs are allowed course familiarization
- Scoring: 15 points per obstacle, except the pause table, which is 20 points
- Timing: 2 yards per second plus 5 seconds
- Faults: Three major faults per obstacle allowed
- Point deductions include:
  - 1 point is deducted for each second overtime
  - 5 points are deducted for major faults (missed contacts, fly-offs, off-courses, failure to complete obstacle while committed, overhandling, breaking the plane of the obstacle)
  - 1–3 points are deducted for minor faults (incorrect entry, tick on the bar, harsh commands)
  - Elimination includes:
  - Knocked down bars
  - Walked over broad jump
  - Excessive handling
  - Handler touching the dog

> **TIP: UKC Faults**
>
> UKC stresses handling and control above speed. The judge may call "fault" for handling errors, missed contacts, or incorrectly performed obstacles. If the judge calls "fault," the handler must have the dog perform the obstacle again. The handler has up to three faults per obstacle in AGI, two faults per obstacle in AGII, and no faults allowed in AGIII.

- Excusals include:
  - Dog leaving the course area
  - Out-of-control dog
  - Exceeding maximum course time
  - Fouling the ring (urinating, defecating, or vomiting)

Agility II
- Total score is 200 points
- Minimum qualifying score is 170 points
- 16 obstacles as defined by AGII rules
- Dogs are allowed course familiarization
- Scoring: 15 points per obstacle, except the pause box, which is 20 points
- Timing: 2 yards per second plus 5 seconds.
- Faults: two major faults per obstacle allowed.
- Point deductions include:
  - 1 point is deducted for each second overtime
  - 5 points are deducted for major faults (missed contacts, fly-offs, off-courses, failure to complete obstacle while committed, overhandling, breaking the plane of the obstacle)
  - 1–3 points are deducted for minor faults (incorrect entry, tick on the bar, harsh commands)

UKC Classes

Class	Who May Enter	Prerequisites
Agility I	Any dog without a title	none
Agility II	Any dog without a title (but must first complete its U-AGI title before receiving the U-AGII title).	none
Agility III	Dog with a U-ACH title	Agility Champion Title

UKC Height at Withers	Jump Height
Size Division 1 (14 inches and under)	8 inches
Size Division 2 (20 inches and under)	14 inches
Size Division 3 (Over 20 inches)	20 inches

UKC Titles

Title	Abbreviation	Requirements
Agility I	U-AGI	Completion of 3 AGI legs with qualifying score
Agility II	U-AGII	Completion of 3 AGII legs with qualifying score and an U-AGI title (may be run concurrently with AGI)
Agility Champion	U-ACH	U-AGII title and 100 points accumulated from both AGI and AGII classes with at least 40 points obtained from AGII • 200 score—10 points • 199 score—6 points • 198 score—4 points • 197 score—2 points • 196 score—1 point
Agility Champion Excellent	U-ACHX	5 qualifying scores in the Agility III class and a U-ACH

- Elimination includes:
  - Knocked down bars
  - Walked over broad jump
  - Excessive handling
  - Handler touching the dog
- Excusals include:
  - Dog leaving the course area
  - Out-of-control dog
  - Exceeding maximum course time
  - Fouling the ring (urinating, defecating, or vomiting)

Agility III
- Total score is 200 points
- Minimum qualifying score is 196 points
- 16 obstacles as defined by AGIII rules

- Dogs are allowed course familiarization
- Scoring: 15 points per non-hurdle obstacle, 10 points per hurdle obstacle, except the pause box or pause table, which is 20 points
- Timing: 2 yards per second plus 5 seconds
- Faults: one major fault per obstacle allowed
- Point deductions include:
  - 1 point is deducted for each second overtime
  - 5 points are deducted for major faults (missed contacts, fly-offs, off-courses, failure to complete obstacle while committed, overhandling, breaking the plane of the obstacle)
  - 1–3 points are deducted for minor faults (incorrect entry, tick on the bar, harsh commands)
- Elimination includes:
  - Knocked down bars
  - Walked over broad jump
  - Excessive handling
  - Handler touching the dog
- Excusals include:
  - Dog leaving the course area
  - Out-of-control dog
  - Exceeding maximum course time
  - Fouling the ring (urinating, defecating, or vomiting)

USDAA

The Classes

USDAA has three programs for obtaining titles: the Championship Program, Performance Program, and the Junior Handler Program. The Championship Program is the original USDAA competition standards based on international competitive rules, whereas, the Performance Program has lower jump heights, lower A-frame, and slower times than the Championship Program. The Junior Handler Program is a special competition program for children up to 18 years old to compete with their dogs. USDAA no longer has a Veterans class, as it is now replaced by the Performance Program.

Within the Championship Program, there are a variety of classes. The beginning handler competes in the standard classes in Starters, if she has never put a USDAA agility title on a dog. Otherwise, she competes in Novice. (Starters is the equivalent of Novice A in AKC agility.) Titling in nonstandard classes within USDAA are reserved for Masters level, but nonstandard classes are offered to lower levels in Championship and Performance programs. A proficient dog may earn Master's titles in Jumpers, Gamblers, Relay, and Snooker. An Agility Dog Champion is a dog that has earned all the Masters class titles, including the additional standard class qualifications.

The Judging Standards

Starters/Novice
- 14–16 obstacles
- Timing: 2.0–2.25 yards per second (varies by jump height)
- Faults include:
  - 5 faults for each off-course
  - 5 faults for knocked down bars
  - 5 faults for missed contact zones
  - 0 faults for first missed pole (must correct and perform weaves correctly)
  - 20 faults for missing an obstacle
  - 5 faults for fly-off

- 5 faults for failure to clear jump span
- 5 faults for touching wishing well base
- 5 faults for handler or outside assistance
- Elimination includes:
  - Excessive handling
  - Handler or outside assistance
  - Omission of an obstacle
  - Running the wrong course with the four paw rule in effect
- Excusals include:
- Dog leaving the course area
- Out-of-control dog
- Exceeding maximum course time
- Fouling the ring (urinating, defecating, or vomiting)
- Failure to abide by the four paw rule
- Poor sportsmanship, including verbal or physical abuse of judge or ring stewards
- Verbal or physical abuse of dog

National agility trials.

USDAA Classes

Class	Who May Enter	Prerequisites
Champion Program		
Starters	Any dog without a title and handler who has never put a title on a dog	None
Novice	Any dog without a title and a handler who has put an agility title on a dog	None
Advanced	Dog with an AD	Agility Dog title
Masters	Dog with an AAD	Advanced Agility Dog title
Masters Gambler	Dog with an AAD	Advanced Agility Dog title or 2 AAD Gamblers legs
Masters Snooker	Dog with an AAD	Advanced Agility Dog title or 2 AAD Snooker legs
Masters Jumpers	Dog with an AAD	Advanced Agility Dog title or 2 AAD Jumpers legs
Masters Relay	Dog with an AAD	Advanced Agility Dog title or 2 AAD Relay legs
Agility Dog Champion	Dog with MAD, GM, JM, RM, and SM	All possible Masters titles
Performance Program		
Performance Dog I	Any dog without a Performance Dog I title	None
Performance Dog II	Dog with a PDI/ AD	Performance Dog I/Agility Dog title
Performance Dog III	Dog with a PDII/ AAD	Performance Dog II/Advanced Agility Dog title
Performance III Jumper	Dog with a PDII/ AAD	Performance Dog II title or dog with 2 PII Jumpers legs
Performance III Gambler	Dog with a PDII/ AAD	Performance Dog II title or dog with 2 PII Gamblers legs
Performance III Snooker	Dog with a PDII/ AAD	Performance Dog II title or dog with 2 PII Snooker legs

USDAA Classes (continued)

Class	Who May Enter	Prerequisites
Junior Handler		
Beginner's Agility Class	Any dog without a title and a handler 18 years or younger, and handler has passed a written rules test	JB
Elementary Agility Class	Dog with JB certificate and a handler 18 years or younger	JE certificate
Intermediate Agility Class	Dog with JE certificate and a handler 18 years or younger	JI certificate
Senior Agility Class	Dog with JI certificate and a handler 18 years or younger	JS certificate

USDAA Championship Height at Withers	Jump Height
12 inches and under	12 inches
16 inches and under	16 inches
21 inches and under	22 inches
Over 21 inches	26 inches

USDAA Performance Height at Withers	Jump Height
12 inches and under	8 inches
16 inches and under	12 inches
21 inches and under	16 inches
Over 21 inches	22 inches

USDAA Junior Height at Withers	Jump Height
12 inches and under	6 or 8 inches
16 inches and under	12 inches
21 inches and under	16 or 18 inches
Over 21 inches	22 or 24 inches

USDAA Titles

Your dog can earn the following titles in USDAA Agility:

Title	Abbreviation	Requirements
Agility Dog	AD	Completion of 3 Starters/Novice Standard legs with qualifying score under 2 judges
Advanced Agility Dog	AAD	Completion of 3 Advanced Standard legs with qualifying score and an AD under 2 judges
Master Agility Dog	MAD	Completion of 3 Master Standard legs with qualifying score and an AAD, plus qualifying scores in Gamblers competition, pairs or team relay, Jumpers, and Snooker competition
Jumpers Master	JM	Completion of 5 Jumpers legs with qualifying score and an AAD
Gamblers Master	GM	Completion of 5 Gamblers legs with qualifying score and an AAD
Snooker Master	SM	Completion of 5 Snookers legs with qualifying score and an AAD
Relay Master	RM	Completion of 5 Relays legs with qualifying score and an AAD
Agility Dog Champion	ADCH	Completion of all Masters Level titles
Agility Top Ten	ATT	Title depends on placement within the year at the Masters level
Performance Dog I	PDI	Completion of 3 Performance I legs with qualifying score
Performance Dog II	PDII	Completion of 3 Performance II legs with qualifying score and a PDI
Performance Dog III	PDIII	Completion of 3 Performance III legs with qualifying score and a PDII
Performance Jumper	PJ	Completion of 5 Jumpers legs with qualifying score and a PDII
Performance Gambler	PG	Completion of 5 Gamblers legs with qualifying score and a PDII
Performance Snooker	PS	Completion of 5 Snookers legs with qualifying score and a PDII
Accomplished Performance Dog	APD	Completion of PDIII, PJ, PG, and PS titles plus 4 additional qualifying scores at the PDIII class
JH Beginners Agility Class	JB	Completion of one clean run at the JH-Beginners level

USDAA Titles (continued)

Title	Abbreviation	Requirements
JH Elementary Agility Class	JE	Completion of two clean runs at the JH-Elementary level
JH Intermediate Agility Class	JI	Completion of three clean runs at the JH-Intermediate level
JH Senior Agility Class	JS	Completion of three clean runs at the JH-Senior level

Advanced

- 17–20 obstacles
- Timing: 2.4–2.55 yards per second (varies by jump height)
- Faults include:
  - 5 faults for each runout/refusal on contact obstacles
  - 20 faults for each off-course
  - 5 faults for knocked down bars
  - 5 faults for missed contact zones
  - 5 faults for first occurrence of missed pole
  - 20 faults for missing an obstacle
  - 5 faults for fly-off
  - 5 faults for failure to clear jump span
  - 5 faults for touching wishing well base
  - 5 faults for handler or outside assistance
- Elimination includes:
  - Excessive handling
  - Three refusals/runouts
  - Handler or outside assistance
  - Omission of an obstacle
  - Running the wrong course with the four paw rule in effect
- Excusals include:
  - Dog leaving the course area
  - Out-of-control dog
  - Exceeding maximum course time
  - Fouling the ring (urinating, defecating, or vomiting)
  - Failure to abide by the four paw rule
  - Poor sportsmanship, including verbal or physical abuse of judge or ring stewards
  - Verbal or physical abuse of dog

Masters (Includes Gamblers, Snooker, Relay, and Jumpers)

- Gamblers and Snooker are point accumulation games. If a dog faults on an obstacle, she doesn't get the points for that obstacle, or the dog is eliminated.
- 17–20 obstacles
- Timing: 2.65–2.85 yards per second (depending on height)
- Faults include:
  - 5 points are deducted for each runout/refusal
  - 5 points deduction for knocked down bars
  - 5 points deduction for missed contact zones
  - 5 points deduction for first occurrence of missed pole
  - 5 point deduction for fly-off
  - 5 point deduction for failure to clear jump span
  - 5 point deduction for touching wishing well base

- 5 point deduction for handler or outside assistance
- Elimination includes:
  - Excessive handling
  - Three refusals/runouts
  - Handler or outside assistance
  - Omission of an obstacle
  - Off-course
  - Running the wrong course with the four paw rule in effect
- Excusals include:
  - Dog leaving the course area
  - Out-of-control dog
  - Exceeding maximum course time

- Fouling the ring (urinating, defecating, or vomiting)
- Failure to abide by the one paw rule
- Poor sportsmanship, including verbal or physical abuse of judge or ring stewards
- Verbal or physical abuse of dog

Performance I
- 14–16 obstacles
- Timing: 2.0–2.25 yards per second (varies by jump height)
- Faults include:
  - 5 faults for each off-course

Agility is open to all competitors with all abilities.

- 5 faults for knocked down bars
- 5 faults for missed contact zones
- 0 faults for first missed pole (must correct and perform weaves correctly)
- 20 faults for missing an obstacle
- 5 faults for fly-off
- 5 faults for failure to clear jump span
- 5 faults for touching wishing well base
- 5 faults for handler or outside assistance
- Elimination includes:
  - Excessive handling
  - Handler or outside assistance
  - Omission of an obstacle
  - Running the wrong course with the four paw rule in effect
- Excusals include:
  - Dog leaving the course area
  - Out-of-control dog
  - Exceeding maximum course time
  - Fouling the ring (urinating, defecating, or vomiting)
  - Failure to abide by the four paw rule
  - Poor sportsmanship, including verbal or physical abuse of judge or ring stewards
  - Verbal or physical abuse of dog

Performance II

- 17–20 obstacles
- Timing: 2.4–2.55 yards per second (varies by jump height)
- Faults include:
  - 5 faults for each runout/refusal on contact obstacles
  - 20 faults for each off-course
  - 5 faults for knocked down bars
  - 5 faults for missed contact zones
  - 5 faults for first occurrence of missed pole
  - 20 faults for missing an obstacle
  - 5 faults for fly-off

- 5 faults for failure to clear jump span
- 5 faults for touching wishing well base
- 5 faults for handler or outside assistance
- Elimination includes:
  - Excessive handling
  - Three refusals/runouts
  - Handler or outside assistance
  - Omission of an obstacle
  - Running the wrong course with the four paw rule in effect
- Excusals include:
  - Dog leaving the course area
  - Out-of-control dog
  - Exceeding maximum course time
  - Fouling the ring (urinating, defecating, or vomiting)
  - Failure to abide by the four paw rule
  - Poor sportsmanship, including verbal or physical abuse of judge or ring stewards
  - Verbal or physical abuse of dog

Performance III (Includes Gamblers, Snooker, and Jumpers)

- Gamblers and Snooker are point accumulation games. If a dog faults on an obstacle, she doesn't get the points for that obstacle, or the dog is eliminated.
- 17–20 obstacles
- Timing: 2.65–2.85 yards per second (depending on height)
- Faults include:
  - 5 points are deducted for each runout/refusal
  - 5 points deduction for knocked down bars
  - 5 points deduction for missed contact zones
  - 5 points deduction for first occurrence of missed pole
  - 5 point deduction for fly-off

Training for the UKC hoop tunnel.

- 5 point deduction for failure to clear jump span
- 5 point deduction for touching wishing well base
- 5 point deduction for handler or outside assistance
- Elimination includes:
  - Excessive handling
  - Three refusals/runouts
  - Handler or outside assistance
  - Omission of an obstacle
  - Off-course
  - Running the wrong course with the four paw rule in effect
- Excusals include:
  - Dog leaving the course area
  - Out-of-control dog
  - Exceeding maximum course time
  - Fouling the ring (urinating, defecating, or vomiting)
  - Failure to abide by the one paw rule
  - Poor sportsmanship, including verbal or physical abuse of judge or ring stewards
  - Verbal or physical abuse of dog

Junior Handler—Beginning Agility
- 10 obstacles (horseshoe, M, or S pattern)
- Timing: 60 seconds
- Nonqualification includes:
  - Any faults
  - Excessive handling
  - Handler or outside assistance
  - Multiple omission of obstacles
  - Running the wrong course with the four paw rule in effect
- Excusals include:
  - Dog leaving the course area
  - Out-of-control dog
  - Exceeding maximum course time
  - Fouling the ring (urinating, defecating, or vomiting)
  - Failure to abide by the four paw rule
  - Poor sportsmanship, including verbal or physical abuse of judge or ring stewards
  - Verbal or physical abuse of dog

Junior Handler—Elementary Agility
- 12–14 obstacles (horseshoe or S pattern)
- Starter dogs are allowed contact familiarization

USDAA discontinued the Veterans Program as of March 31, 1999 in favor of the Performance Program. You may still see some Veterans titles on dogs. These include: Veteran Agility Dog (VAD), Advanced Veteran Agility Dog (AVAD), Masters Veteran Agility Dog (MVAD), Veteran Gambler (VG), Veteran Snooker (VS), Veteran Jumper (VJ), and Veteran Performance Dog (VPD). The Veterans class was only open to dogs seven or more years old. Some local clubs may offer their own veterans awards to older dogs competing in Championship or Performance programs.

- Timing: 75 seconds
- Nonqualification includes:
  - Any faults
  - Excessive handling
  - Handler or outside assistance
  - Omission of any obstacle
  - Running the wrong course with the four paw rule in effect
- Excusals include:
  - Dog leaving the course area
  - Out-of-control dog
  - Exceeding maximum course time
  - Fouling the ring (urinating, defecating, or vomiting)
  - Failure to abide by the four paw rule
  - Poor sportsmanship, including verbal or physical abuse of judge or ring stewards
  - Verbal or physical abuse of dog

Junior Handler—Senior Agility

- 13–15 obstacles (a little more challenging than a figure 8)

- Timing: 2 yards per second; cannot exceed 75 seconds
- Nonqualification includes:
  - Any faults
  - Excessive handling
  - Handler or outside assistance
  - Omission of any obstacle
  - Running the wrong course with the four paw rule in effect
- Excusals include:
  - Dog leaving the course area
  - Out-of-control dog
  - Exceeding maximum course time
  - Fouling the ring (urinating, defecating, or vomiting)
  - Failure to abide by the four paw rule
  - Poor sportsmanship, including verbal or physical abuse of judge or ring stewards
  - Verbal or physical abuse of dog

National Competitions

The fun of agility does not stop at titles, although your dog could conceivably work towards every possible title available in all four organizations for the rest of his life. Every year, each major organization holds a national agility trial where top dogs compete for rankings. These events are spectacular, going beyond the simple agility trial. Dogs from across the country come to compete at these trials. The entry requirements are stringent. For USDAA's Grand Prix of Dog Agility, for example, the dog must go through regional, semifinals, and then finals before being accepted into the Championships.

USDAA has the Dog Agility Masters Team Championships and the Dog Agility Steeplechase Jumpers Championships. Both require prequalification in regional tournaments.

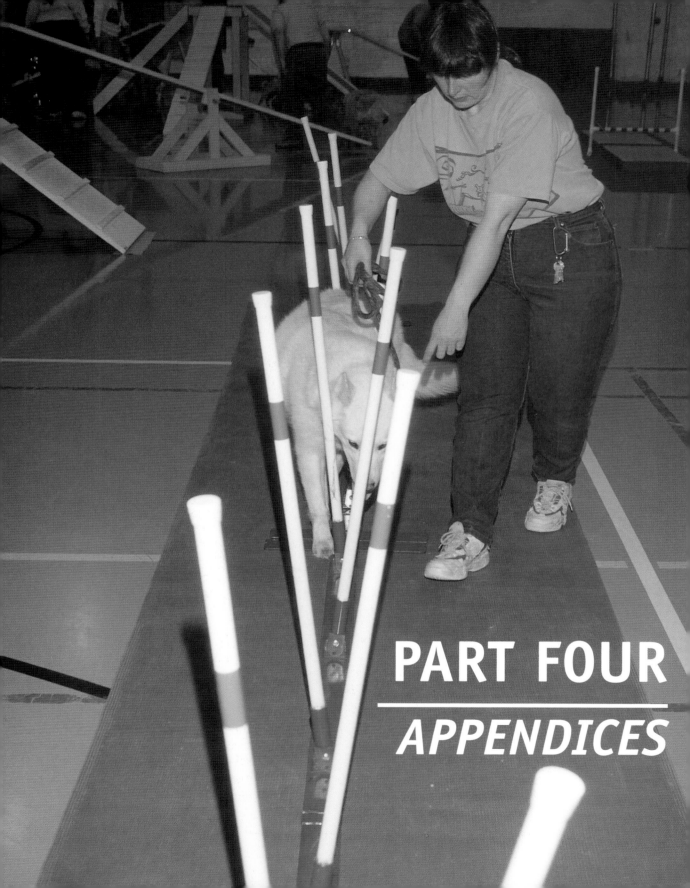

PART FOUR

APPENDICES

Appendix A

Addresses of National Agility Organizations

National Agility Organizations

American Kennel Club (AKC)
5580 Centerview Drive
Raleigh, NC 27606-3390
(919) 233-9767
www.akc.org/
e-mail: info@akc.org

North American Dog Agility Council (NADAC)
HCR 2, Box 277
St. Maries, ID 83861
(208) 689-3803
www.nadac.com/
e-mail:nadack9@aol.com

United Kennel Club (UKC)
100 East Kilgore Road
Kalamazoo, MI 49001-5593
www.ukcdogs.com/

United States Dog Agility Association (USDAA)
PO Box 850955
Richardson, TX 75085-0955
(972) 231-9700
Information Line: (888) AGILITY
www.usdaa.com/
e-mail: info@usdaa.com

Agility Association of Canada (AAC)
RR #2
Lucan, Ontario
N0N2J0
(519) 657-7636

Australian Shepherd Club of America (ASCA)
6091 East State Highway 21
Bryan, TX 77803-9652
(409) 778-1082
e-mail: asca@mail.myraid.net

Health Registries

Orthopedic Foundation for Animals
2300 Nifong Boulevard
Columbia, MO 65201
(314) 442-0418

Canine Eye Registration Foundation
Department of Veterinary Clinical Science
School of Veterinary Medicine
Purdue University
West Lafayette, IN 47907
(765) 494-8179; Fax: (765) 494-9981

Appendix B

Agility References

Books and Periodicals

Periodicals

Clean Run
Monica Percival and Linda Mechlenburg
35 Walnut Street
Turner Falls, MA 01376
(413) 863-8308
www.cleanrun.com/
e-mail: info@cleanrun.com

Dog Fancy Magazine
PO Box 6050
Mission Viejo, CA 92690

Dog World
29 N. Wacker Drive
Chicago, IL 60606

Rulebooks for the Various Agility Organizations

Exhibitor's Handbook for Rules Governing North American Dog Agility Council Sanctioned Trials
NADAC, HCR 2, Box 277
St. Maries, ID 83861
Available online and through NADAC.
(208) 689-3803
www.nadac.com/

Official Rules and Regulations of the United States Dog Agility Association, Inc.
Portions available online. Full text available through USDAA.
(972) 231-9700
Information Line: (888) AGILITY
www.usdaa.com/

Regulations for Agility Trials
Available online or through AKC.
(919) 233-9780
www.akc.org/

Agility Rules, Special Edition
Available online or through UKC.
(616) 343-9020
www.ukcdogs.com/

Agility Books and General Reference

Alderton, David. *The Dog Care Manual.* Hauppauge, NY: Barron's Educational Series, Inc., 1986.

American Kennel Club. *The Complete Dog Book, 19th Edition, Revised.* New York: Howell Book House, 1997.

Baer, Ted. *Communicating with Your Dog.* Hauppauge, NY: Barron's Educational Series, Inc., 1989.

Bailey, Gwen. *The Well-Behaved Dog.* Hauppauge, NY: Barron's Educational Series, Inc., 1998.

Benjamin, Carol Lea. *Second-Hand Dog.* New York: Howell Book House, 1988.

Carlson, Delbert G. DVM, and Griffin, James M. MD. *The Dog Owner's Home Veterinary Handbook.* New York: Howell Book House, 1992.

Coffman, Howard D. *The Dry Dog Food Reference.* Nashua, NH: Pig Dog Press, 1995.

Collins, Donald R. DVM. *The Collins Guide to Dog Nutrition.* New York: Howell Book House, 1987.

Daniel, Julie. *Enjoying Dog Agility.* Wilsonville, OR: Doral Publishing, 1991.

Elliot, Rachel Page. *The New Dogsteps.* New York: Howell Book House, 1983.

Gilbert, Edward M. Jr. and Brown, Thelma R. *K-9 Structure and Terminology.* New York: Howell Book House, 1995.

Hinchcliff, Kenneth W. BVSc, MS, Ph.D., Diplomate ACVIM, Reinhart, Gregory A. Ph.D., Reynolds, Arleigh J. *Performance Dog Nutrition.* Dayton, Ohio: The Iams Company, 1999.

Holst, Phyllis A. MS, DVM. *Canine Reproduction: A Breeder's Guide.* Loveland, CO: Alpine Publications, 1985.

Hutchins, Jim. *HOGA Agility, Do-It-Yourself Plans for Constructing Dog Agility Articles.* Jackson, MS: HOGA Agility, 1999.

James, Ruth B. DVM. *The Dog Repair Book.* Mills, Wyoming: Alpine Press, 1990.

Klever, Ulrich. *The Complete Book of Dog Care.* Hauppauge, NY: Barron's Educational Series, Inc., 1989.

Merck and Co. *The Merck Veterinary Manual, Seventh Edition.* Whitehouse Station, NJ: Merck and Co., Inc., 1991.

O'Neil, Jacqueline. *All About Agility.* New York: Howell Book House, 1998.

Papurt, M. L. *Saved! A Guide to Success with Your Shelter Dog.* Hauppauge, NY: Barron's Educational Series, Inc., 1997.

Pryor, Karen. *Don't Shoot the Dog! The New Art of Teaching and Training.* New York: Bantam Doubleday Dell, 1999.

Ralston Purina Company. *Purina's Complete Guide to Nutrition, Care, and Health for Your Dog and Cat.* St. Louis, MO: Ralston Purina Company.

Rice, Dan, DVM. *The Complete Book of Dog Breeding.* Hauppauge, NY: Barron's Educational Series, Inc., 1996.

Simmons-Moake, Jane. *Agility Training, The Fun Sport for all Dogs.* New York: Howell Book House: 1992.

Smith, Cheryl S. *Pudgy Pooch, Picky Pooch.* Hauppauge, NY: Barron's Educational Series, Inc., 1998.

Smith, Cheryl S. and Tauton, Stephanie J. *The Trick is in the Training.* Hauppauge, NY: Barron's Educational Series, Inc., 1998.

Streitferdt, Uwe. *Healthy Dog, Happy Dog.* Hauppauge, NY: Barron's Educational Series, Inc., 1994.

Wrede, Barbara J. *Civilizing Your Puppy, Second Edition,* Hauppauge, NY: Barron's Educational Series, Inc., 1997.

Zink, M. Chris, DVM, Ph.D. Peak Performance, *Coaching the Canine Athlete.* New York: Howell Book House, 1992.

Agility on the Internet: E-mail Lists and Websites

Agility and Working Organizations, Hip and Eye Registries

AKC Website
www.akc.org/

CERF Website
www.vet.purdue.edu/~yshen/cerf.html

Clicker Training Website
http://clickertraining.com/

The Dogpatch (has an excellent agility events search engine)
www.dogpatch.org/

North American Dog Agility Council
www.nadac.com/

OFA Website
www.offa.org/

UKC Website
www.ukcdogs.com/

United States Dog Agility Association
www.usdaa.com/

AGILEDOGS E-mail List
Send the following command to
LISTSERV@APPLE.EASE.LSOFT.COM
in the body of the message:
SUBSCRIBE AGILEDOGS-L your-name-here
Where your-name-here is your actual name.

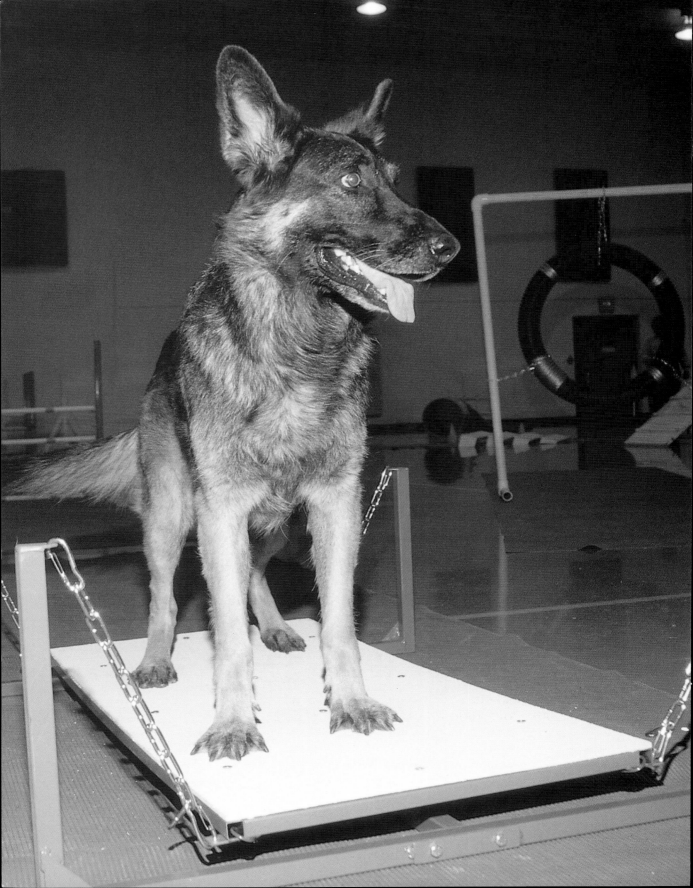

Appendix **D**

Agility and Obedience Equipment Suppliers

The Agility Connection
PO Box 901992
Kansas City, MO 64190-1882
(887) 735-9652
http://www.theagilityconnection.com/
e-mail: skihusky@aol.com

Agility Of Course
Box 567M RD #1
Afton, NY 13730
http://members.aol.com/psbdrcolli
e-mail: psbdrcolli@aol.com

Agility Works
Vacaville, CA
(707) 448-7577
http://www.agilityworks.com/
e-mail: info@agilityworks.com

Available Plastics (PVC connectors)
PO Box 924
Huntsville, AL 35804
(800) 633-7212
http://www.genovaproducts.com/
e-mail: genova@genovaproducts.com

Doggy Gym
1965 Old Dominon Dr.
Atlanta, GA 30350-4616
(770) 394-5697
http://www.doggygym.com/
e-mail: dog5019@doggygym.com

J and J Dog Supplies
PO Box 1517
Galesburg, IL 61402
(800) 642-2050
http://www.jandjdog.com/
e-mail: jandjdog@galesburg.net

MAX 200
114 Beach St., Bldg 5
Rockaway, NJ 07866
(800) 446-2920
http://www.max200.com/

Northwest Agility Products
846 W. Smith Rd
Bellingham, WA 98226
www.nwagility.com/
e-mail: info@nwagility.com

PTG Furniture Grade PVC Supply
(PVC Connectors)
5311 E. Colonial Drive
Orlando, FL 32807
dpainc.com/ptg2/
e-mail: jsoakes@mindspring.com

The PVC Store (PVC/PVC connectors)
5020 Beechmont Drive
Huntsville, AL 35811
(256) 859-4927
www.thepvcstore.com/
e-mail: info@thepvcstore.com

Toys-R-Us (practice tunnel)
(888) 869-7932
www.toysrus.com/

United States Plastics Corporation
(PVC connectors)
1390 Wenbrecht Road
Lima, OH 45801-3196
(800) 537-9724
www.usplastic.com/
e-mail: usp@usplastic.com

U.S. Toy Company/Constructive Playthings
(practice tunnels)
13201 Arrington Road
Grandview, MO 64030
(800) 448-4115
www.constplay.com/

Appendix **E**

Metric Conversion Table

Converting from English to Metric

1 in.	=	25.4 mm
1 in.	=	2.54 cm
1 ft.	=	0.3 m
1 yd.	=	0.91 m
1 mi.	=	1.61 m

Converting from Metric to English

1 mm	=	0.039 in.
1 cm	=	0.39 in.
1 m	=	3.28 ft.
1 m	=	1.09 yd.
1 km	=	0.62 mi.
1 l	=	1.06 qt.
1 l	=	0.26 gal.
1 g	=	0.04 oz.
1 kg	=	2.2 lb.

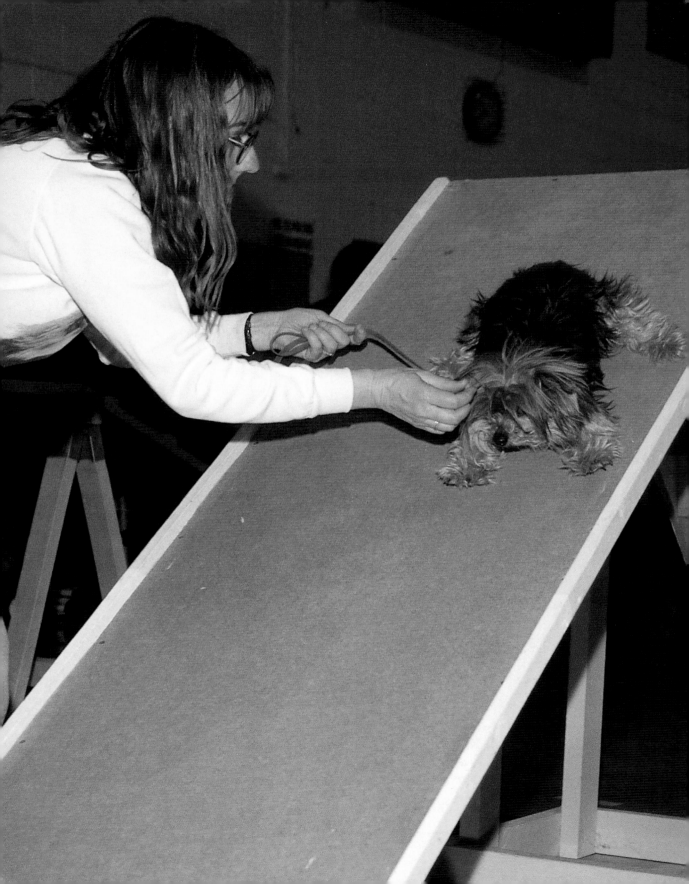

Index